PREFACE

The evolution of printmaking technology can be seen as a pattern which has repeated itself with each printmaking process. First, a process fulfills the need for producing pictures which duplicate art work inexpensively and quickly. With knowledge and practice, control is achieved to the point whereby the method can make possible remarkable imitations of other art media. Finally, with acquired confidence, the images begin to lose some of their emulative quality and evolve an identity characteristic of the unique qualities of the particular process. Screen Printing finds itself at this challenging stage in its development.

As public exposure to art has grown, the need for new forms has grown with it. Structures drained of their impact by repeated use become stylistic clichés. Hence, heretofore unavailable materials and methods developed by contemporary technology for visual communication form a rich aesthetic reservoir which should be tapped. With this book we hope to do just that. We will discuss the how and why of screen printing, starting with basic and traditional stencil processes and progressing to the more advanced principles and techniques of photographic stencil making.

The philosophical premise of this book is that technical efficiency is the means to an end in creative expression. We trust that by exploring and experiencing the creative possibilities of screen printing, the reader will develop the ability to use this remarkable medium with maximum effectiveness. Our motivation stems from the belief that the knowledge of what a medium can do and the ability to do it are the hallmarks of artistic virtuosity.

ACKNOWLEDGEMENTS

We are indebted to many persons who have shared experience and ideas with us. Here we wish to thank them—colleagues, teachers, friends—for what they have contributed in countless ways. We owe much to students, both present and past, who taught us at least as much as we taught them. Special acknowl... ay whose frienc ... a guiding force ... oject, Arthur A ... lis support and c... ...his book possible. We sincerely appreciate the skill Fred Kaupp brought to the book's design and layout. Steven Maiorano deserves our warmest thanks for pitching in and adding his considerable technical abilities to this effort. It is impossible to fully express our gratitude to Neil Scholl for his contribution. His involvement extended far beyond laboring patiently, diligently and with great sensitivity to produce all the photographs and illustrations. To these and many others, as well as the unseen forces that influence our lives, we say—Thank you!

For the most precious contribution, we are indebted to Richard, our son, for the time he sacrificed that rightfully should have been his—and for understanding. We gratefully dedicate this book to this very special person.

December, 1977
New York City

1

CHAPTER 1

In spite of the fact that definitions have often served to replace sleeping pills for readers, some twenty-four entries following "print" in Webster's New World Dictionary convinced us that it was necessary to establish a frame of reference for the reader. Mr. Webster concludes that to print is to make a mark on or in a surface. Since this definition applies to most any form of two-dimensional representation, we turned to contemporary usage which describes printing as a technical procedure for producing numerous identical copies of a single work. Therefore, the Gutenberg Bible, a two-dollar bill, the senior class photo, your Camp Iroquois "T" shirt and the book you are reading are examples of printing! They each satisfy the principle of printing as reproduction. But, you are thinking, they all look so different! Of course they do, because each was created by a different printing process. There are five basic printing processes: relief (Gutenberg Bible), intaglio (two-dollar bill), photography (senior class photo), planography (this book) and stencil ("T" shirt). Each of these printing methods involves the transfer of ink to a surface, except photography which uses the medium of light. The way each process achieves this transfer is what makes it unique.

Of the five major printing processes, the relief or "raised surface" method of printing is probably the most familiar and simplest. It may also be the oldest, if we consider the first cave man who wiped his smudged hand on a surface and saw his fingerprint as the accidental, unheralded discoverer of relief printing!

Relief printing is defined as the transfer of ink from the raised surface of a material, like a rubber stamp inked on a pad and then pressed against paper to leave F-R-A-G-I-L-E. Interestingly, that rubber stamp and the Gutenberg Bible share a history.

We know that duplicate printing could not have come into existence without the use of paper—parchment being too rigid and papyrus too brittle for that purpose. Since papermaking originated in China, it was possible for that country to pioneer in the art of duplicate printing. Chinese multiple printing began as seals impressed on documents and later for Buddhist inspired prayers, the multiplication of which by printing was believed to increase the chances of gaining entry to Paradise. By about the 9th Century in China and the 15th Century in Europe, printmaking for the masses began to flourish. The needs which fostered reproduction have essentially remained the same. The decline of the aristocrat and the rise of the merchant in the Orient as well as in the West brought with it the making of prints for the masses. The "patron-prince" was forced by economic necessity to withdraw support of the artist. This meant that an artist who did not choose to starve had to offer eye-catching pictures of popular subjects at bargain prices. The artist had to aim at quantity production and quick turnover to make up for low prices. By the end of the 18th Century, the Japanese had established many of our contemporary principles and traditions of printmaking. A printmaking project employed the unique skills of a team of artist-craftsmen—the designer, the block cutter and the printer. Needless to add, the success of a printmaking enterprise depended, as it does today, on the contribution of each individual to this collaboration.

The principles of relief printing remain unchanged. In creating his printing block, be it wood or linoleum, the artist decides which areas will be inked and then cuts away those areas which will not be inked. This leaves those parts to be printed higher or in relief, so that when inked and placed over paper, these relief areas of the block create the image.

Although the delicate soft color woodblock prints of Japan have profoundly influenced Western art, the tradition of black and white block prints has never been replaced. In the early 20th Century, the German Expressionists achieved an aesthetic impact of great significance through the woodblock print. The forms in these prints result directly from the form of the wood grain itself. Furthermore, within these intense and organically derived planes one detects the working of the gouge itself on the block. Through technique, a forcefulness of expression rarely equaled by other mediums was achieved.

Relief printing as it is now practiced continues to be a medium of direct impact of color planes.

It should be noted that because of the position of the paper as it receives the ink from the block, what reads right to left on the block will read left to right on the paper. This is known as mirror image and requires the artist to plan ahead knowingly.

The principle of intaglio printing is just the opposite of relief printing. An image is cut into a metal, wooden or lucite plate and then ink is rubbed into these incised lines. The image is printed by pressing paper into the inked incisions. Engraving and etching are intaglio processes.

Engraving is carried out on plates of copper, steel or zinc. Burins are used to cut into the plate, making V-shaped channels. The deeper a line is engraved, the wider it becomes and the heavier it prints. After engraving, the plate is cleaned and heated, then the engraved lines are filled with ink and the surface wiped clean. The plate is centered, face up on the bed of a heavy press. Dampened paper is laid on top of the plate and blankets of felt are placed over the paper. When a heavy roller is pulled over the plate, paper and felt, the pressure forces the damp paper into the incised lines and ink is transferred to the paper as slightly raised lines.

Paper money, as well as wedding invitations and calling cards are common examples of engravings. If you look closely at a dollar bill with a magnifying glass, you will see some of the fine textures—cross hatching, dots, dashes, parallel lines—that are made possible by this process.

Drypoints are superficially only slightly different from engravings. Lines are cut into plates with needle-like points made of sharpened steel or diamond or ruby. These make a finer indentation than the burin and can create a looser, sketchier line. Also, a drypoint needle throws up tiny, irregular edges of metal called a *burr* that are left on the plate,

while a sharp burin leaves no burr and any left by a dull tool are scraped off. Printing drypoints is similar to printing engravings. Ink is rubbed into the warmed plate—but in wiping the plate some ink is left in the burr, which gives the drypoint its characteristically soft, velvety line. Also, a very thin film of ink is frequently left on the surface to give the background a light tone.

Editions of drypoints are limited in number unless the plate has been coated with steel. Since the burr is worn off by printing, it is the first twenty-five to thirty prints which have the greatest textural richness.

Etchings are not easily distinguished from drypoints. The special qualities of etching become clear as we consider the way in which it is accomplished. First, a plate of copper or zinc is covered with a thin layer of *ground*—a dark, waxy material that is easily penetrated with a metal needle, but is resistant to acid. Using a needle that is blunter than that used for drypoint, the lines to be printed are drawn through the ground. This exposes parts of the plate while not scratching the metal. Then the plate is immersed in an acid bath that eats away the exposed metal. The depth of the lines on the plate which, as we mentioned determines the darkness of the printed lines, is determined by the length of time the plate remains in the acid bath. A single immersion gives lines of equal depth. Variety is achieved by removing the plates from time to time and covering those lines considered deep enough with a stop-out varnish and returning the plate for further biting. The printing is identical to drypoint. There are other intaglio processes used alone or often with other techniques. Among these are aquatints. Aquatints are made by covering a metal plate with rosin dust and heating it. Each rosin particle adheres to the plate as a hardened crystal and the spaces between are etched with acid. Some areas are stopped-out with varnish, while others are exposed to acid. Repeated many times, this can create textured areas that range from almost pure white to pure black.

The eloquence to which line and value can aspire

is associated with prints by Rembrandt. Because he sought black and white virtuosity, it is said that Rembrandt carried a metal plate with him in place of a sketch book, using an etching needle to make his sketches. Upon returning to his studio, he would ink and print the plates. The great master's efforts provide ample testimony to the unique textural and tonal richness made possible by the intaglio process.

Again, in intaglio, the image that appears on the paper is the reverse of the image on the plate.

Planography is more commonly known as lithography. Lithography makes use of the principle of surface or chemical printing. It is based on the antipathy of grease and water rather than on raising or lowering printing surfaces. The process was first introduced by Aloys Senfelder in 1797 who noticed that certain stones had an affinity for both oil and water. He drew on a stone with a greasy substance. When he dampened the stone, the water was repelled from the greasy area. Then, while trying to cover the entire stone with an oil based pigment, Senfelder discovered that the pigment adhered only to the greasy area. He found that the damp parts of the stone would not absorb the oily pigment. When he placed a sheet of paper against the stone and subjected it to pressure, the pigment was transferred to the paper. From this simple discovery the art of lithography grew. Today, certain kinds of zinc and paper plates can be used in place of the stone with excellent results. Lithography is especially suited for works of subtle tonalities, washes and values. It is possible to achieve both linear and tonal effects on the same stone or plate, making it an adaptable color medium. Henri de Toulouse Lautrec found the freedom which lithography allows in the drawing phase admirably suited to his approach. His prints and posters are fine examples of the wide variety of line, texture and shading this medium can produce.

In lithography, as in the other printing mediums discussed, the image is reversed.

Photography is a printing process which produces an image on chemically sensitive paper with the aid of light. Since at least the 10th Century, it has been known that rays of light passing through a pinhole would form an image. The Arabian scholar Alhazen described the effect in detail and told how to view an eclipse of the sun in a *camera obscura* (dark chamber).

The camera obscura is based on the principle that if a darkened room has only one light source—a small round hole in one wall, that the light rays coming through that hole will produce an inverted image on the opposite wall of the scene outside the pinhole wall.

Although the technique of photography is basically simple, it was not until the early 19th Century that the researches of Daguerre, Niepce, Talbot and others brought about the perfection of the photographic print process. That is, the principle of fixing an image on paper, glass or film by purely optical and chemical means and then printing from the negative. The camera can translate whatever it sees in terms of light and dark upon the plate or film. It is believed by some that photography is a precise mechanical process for duplicating human vision. However, this does not take into account that photography is simply another pictorial convention and that the eye of the camera has its own kind of "personality". The camera's diverse-angled lenses and monocular vision produce distortions of "reality" compared to human binocular vision. It has been said that since its operations are mechanical, it cannot be considered an artistic print medium. As we see, *all* print mediums have mechanical elements which the artist has learned to manipulate and control. Certainly, there are more than enough opportunities in the photographic process for the artist to express himself personally: lighting and arrangement of materials, choice of lenses, change of focus, variations in development and printing.

The darkening of certain silver compounds by exposure to light had been observed as early as the 17th Century. Nonetheless, the problem of halting this reaction so that the image would not become totally darkened remained. At the beginning of the 19th Century, Thomas Wedgewood, son of the famed British potter, made negative silhouettes by using leaves and insect wings as stencils. He placed the object on white paper which had been sensitized with silver nitrate, and then exposed it to the sun. The paper darkened where it was exposed to light but was unaffected where it was shielded by the object. Although Wedgewood tried many ways to make these silhouettes permanent when light struck the images, they began to darken like the rest of the coating. Interestingly, although Wedgewood had been working along the right lines by investigating silver compounds, the first permanent picture did not involve silver. What is considered the first photograph was made by Joseph Niepce in 1826. Niepce was a gentleman inventor who had become interested in the new process of lithography. Lithography required that a drawing be hand copied in reverse onto the printing stone. Niepce searched for an automatic method to accomplish this transfer. His search, once begun, extended to an attempt to copy views directly from nature by using the camera obscura. He sought and found a way to fix the camera's image permanently. Although he first experimented with silver chloride, his attention turned to bitumen of Judea, a kind of asphalt that hardened when exposed to light. Niepce dissolved the bitumen in lavender oil and then coated a sheet of pewter with the mixture. He placed the sheet in a camera obscura—pointed through an open window of his courtyard. The exposed area hardened and the unexposed still soft bitumen dissolved, leaving a permanent image. The eight hours of exposure time was so long that the sun moved across the sky and both sides of the courtyard were illuminated. He called this fixed image a heliograph. This was actually a negative image on a metal plate fixed with bitumen and reproducible like a print, by engraving and printing.

After many years of experimenting both with Niepce and alone, it was Louis Daguerre, a French painter, who simplified the process of making pictures permanent and in 1839 introduced the Daguerreotype to the world.

Daguerre was considered a naturalistic painter, one who depicted natural scenes with explicit accuracy. His greatest triumph came when he finally succeeded in having light paint his pictures. The Daguerreotype, made on a silver-plated copper sheet, faithfully recorded and made permanent an image with precise detail and remarkable tonal and textural range. Each plate was, however, a unique positive. The photographic process whereby any number of positives can be printed from one negative was perfected in 1840 by William Henry Fox Talbot, an Englishman. The technique, which he called calotype, from the Greek words for beautiful impression, became the basis of modern photographic chemistry. Talbot used paper, rather than metal for the negative and the positive reproductions; with light-sensitive silver chloride as the image making agent. He fixed the image by washing out all the silver salts unaffected by light with sodium hyposulfite (hypo). The fully developed negative was then placed in contact with another sensitized sheet of paper and exposed to light—a procedure we now know as contact printing.

Beginning with the Daguerreotype, viewers were astounded by the acute clarity with which a photograph could copy. This belief in the camera as a literal recorder gave rise to the still prevalent idea that "the camera does not lie". The photograph, endowed with such psychological strength, became the embodiment of documentary truth. Until photography had come along, printmaking had been assigned to documentation, illustration and reproduction. By relieving printmaking of this role, photography replaced printmaking as the most utilitarian and hence the lowest art in the fine arts hierarchy. This necessitated a new direction and justification for printmaking, thus enabling printmaking to achieve recognition as an independent and creative art form.

In its immediacy, simplicity and imitativeness, we find photography's strengths as well as the reasons for its suffering in recognition as an art. So, too the process of screen printing because it is so adaptable and autographic, instead of being regarded as the most advanced, is accorded the least prestige of all the printmaking processes.

Screen printing is basically a stencil printing process. Stencil printing involves covering the surface to be printed with an impervious material like cardboard or paper into which openings have been cut that reveal parts of the underlying surface. Ink is passed across the stencil which acts as a mask so that when the stencil is removed, only the shapes of the open areas are printed onto the surface below.

The stencil process can be traced back 20,000 years to the caves at Les Eyzies and Lascaux where prints of hands appear on the walls among the reindeer and horse paintings. These prints were stenciled by placing the hand on the wall of the cave and blowing pigments through a reed or hollow bone onto the area left uncovered by the hand. The hand was then removed to reveal the stenciled print. For centuries the stencil was used for applying areas of color to walls, textiles, and furniture. The Egyptians and Greeks used stencils to decorate their pots, fabrics and buildings. Children of Roman times learned the letters of their alphabet by drawing them through lettered cut stencils.

Although intricate designs can be cut in a stencil, there are limitations imposed by the fact that the stencil must hold together. All floating areas must be attached to the body of the stencil by "bridges" so that these bridges have to be accepted as part of the image. This limitation was dealt with by Japanese stencil cutters by attaching hair to the floating areas in a web-like manner. The hair was strong enough to hold the islands in place, yet fine enough to allow the ink to flow around them while being barely visible after the image was printed. The hair was often stretched across a frame in a grid system and the stencil attached to it. From this basic principle of hair being stretched across a frame and a stencil attached to the hair, research and experiment developed the process further. By the beginning of this century, the use of a screen with silk cloth as the stencil carrier had been developed. Today, this screen principle although refined, is essentially the same. The screen consists of a rigid frame on which the fabric is stretched and drawn tight. The stencil is attached to the underside of the fabric or imbedded in the mesh. Ink is forced through the mesh onto the surface below.

Because silk was the earliest material stretched across a frame to create a screen, the process became known as silk screen printing. This term persists despite the fact that most screens in use today are made of synthetic fibers whose stability, consistency and durability are not as subject to atmospheric changes as silk.

Screen printing is undoubtedly the most versatile color medium. Any conceivable color can be screen printed. Screen printing inks are available to create finishes which range from matte to high gloss; in consistencies from transparent to opaque; and only with screen printing can ink be laid down so transparently it is almost invisible, or so thick that it appears to be a collaged element. The unparalleled color and texture versatility, plus the fact that the image does not reverse, makes it by far the most direct and painterly of printing mediums. Also, since screen printing does not involve indirect transfer by extreme pressure as other processes do, it is not confined to paper. Screen printing can be applied to almost any surface—glass, fabric, wood, metal, plastic, to mention but a few. There can be little wonder why it was seized upon by commercial printers, because unlike other techniques, screen printing was first developed as a commercial process. Less than a century ago, the commercial value of screen printing was recognized in the United States, allowing it to grow into a thriving industry. Its unique characteristics made it capable of successfully competing with other printing processes. Screen printing is used on items all around you—wallpaper, bumper stickers, decals, signs, posters, "T" shirts, bottles, cans, highway and traffic signs, shopping bags, penants, boxes, greeting cards and of course, fine arts prints.

Interestingly, screen printing did not become known and used as an artistic medium until quite recently. This was due in part to the secrecy with which commercial screen printers guarded their process. In addition, the fact that no artist lent it the prestige which etching and lithography had acquired added to its "commercial" association and to the delay of its fine arts debut. In 1938, Anthony Velonis, as head of the New York City Graphic Division of the WPA Federal Arts Project, joined with a group of artists to create a program to investigate "silk screen" as a fine art medium. This experiment led to original prints which were exhibited and written about throughout the country. From this beginning, the broad possibilities of this art medium and its promotion to the level of fine art still continues.

Perhaps, it is no accident that the youngest of the printmaking processes is American, if not by birth by adoption. Perhaps, too, its youth, its utilitarian roots, and its nationality make it at once the most exciting print form and the least prominent. In fact, it was probably this self-consciousness which caused the word "serigraphy" to be originated as a term to be applied when referring to screen printing as a fine art. Serigraphy means drawing in silk, as lithography means drawing in stone. Since the phrase, silk-screen printing has been replaced by the more generic term, screen printing, one must consider the application of the term serigraphy as an attempt to confer status by affecting a European association. This appears both inaccurate and self-denying, since, in screen printing, unlike painting, sculpture or the other printing processes, we find an art medium which owes little to Europe, but much to America for its growth and development.

CHAPTER 2

An image printed as a woodcut will not look the same printed as a lithograph. This is not only because of the unique qualities of each medium, but because each requires an artist to work in a different manner. We hope that our survey of the basic printmaking processes has convinced you that prints are physical, as well as visual objects. However, taken by itself, technique is to visual art, what grammar is to literature. It is the underlying form—giving power of art; the "means" by which the "end" is achieved. In part, screen printing has been unexplored as an aesthetic medium because of a lack of up-to-date, thorough, technical information. This book is our attempt to broaden the reader's graphic language by investigating the methods and materials of screen printing. Ultimately, technique must become inextricably interwoven with content to produce a work of art. We have confined ourselves to technical considerations, and leave it to each reader to integrate personal expression uniquely.

We heartily recommend screen printing to both the beginning and advanced artist. Screen printing allows color, line, shape and texture to be presented in almost any conceivable way, and applied to potentially any surface. What more could one want? The basic methods can be learned quickly. Image size is an aesthetic not a technical decision, since large or small sizes can be printed with equal ease. It is the most direct type of printmaking; the image does not reverse when printed. The ability to develop an image which is direct and immediate makes screen printing autographic and "forgiving". However, before exploring the various methods and materials for creating visual imagery, let's look at the printing unit.

One more of the many advantages of screen printing is that it does not require elaborate, mechanical apparatus. The necessary equipment can be simple, quite inexpensive, and portable. The basic printing unit consists of a fabric-covered frame, the screen which is hinged to a baseboard, upon which the printing is done, and a squeegee, with which ink is applied. We will discuss several choices for building or buying each of the components. Based upon our experience, we will include some specific recommendations.

THE SCREEN

The screen is simply a frame over which a mesh material is stretched. Screens may be purchased pre-assembled and stretched with fabric.

Frame: You can buy or make a frame. Beginners are advised to buy wooden frames which are available in a variety of pre-cut sizes (commercial shops use frames made of metal and aluminum as well as wood). These pre-cut strips of frame lumber are

Pre-cut strips are generally constructed with a 45° miter end. This allows corners to be joined with corrugated staples, with nails or with screws. The corners are strengthened by applying waterproof glue before employing one of these physical joining methods.

manufactured in lengths which range from 6″ to 48″ and larger. These lengths are made of lumber with width dimensions from 1⅛″ square to 1½″ x 3½″ depending, of course, on the length of the frame member. The frame members are generally constructed with a 45 degree miter end, which allows the corners to be assembled with corrugated staples, with nails, or with screws. To strengthen the corners, we recommend that waterproof glue be applied before employing any of the physical joining methods. (Note: Waterproof glue is available at hardware stores. It comes in two parts and should be mixed immediately prior to use.) We then suggest using screws for the final fastening.

To construct your own frame, use either clear pine or redwood lumber. The dimensions of the lumber will, of course, depend on the length of the sides of the finished frame. A simple and durable frame system up to 24″ x 24″ with rigid corner joints can be

Pre-cut frame member. These pre-cut strips of lumber are manufactured in lengths from 6″ to 48″ and longer, with width dimensions 1⅛″ square to 1½ x 3½ inch.

made of 1 x 2's made up in strips according to the following directions: Each side of the frame will require two strips of 1 x 2 lumber. One strip should measure the full length desired for the finished side; a second strip must be the length of the side minus double the dimension of the width of the 1 x 2. While this should obviously be 2″ on left and 2″ on right, care must be exercised and measurements taken because 1 x 2's are not always 1 x 2!

The shorter strip is glued and tacked in the center of the longer strip. Follow this procedure until you have constructed four of this kind of frame member. The frame members are then ready to be assembled in a "lap-joint" manner. After applying waterproof glue to the edges and surfaces which will contact each other, the pieces are fitted together. They can be permanently joined with flat-head wood screws of an appropriate length. We urge you to drill holes to accept the screws, this will avoid the possibility of splitting the wood. It is advisable to use at least two flat-head screws to fasten each of the four corners. We consider it essential that the flat-head screws be screwed down so that they are flush with or slightly below the surface of the wood.

To construct your own frame use either clear pine or redwood lumber. Each side of the frame requires two strips of 1 x 2 lumber. One strip should measure the full length desired for the finished side, the second strip should be the length of the side minus double the width of the 1 x 2. The shorter strip is glued in the center of the longer strip. This procedure is followed until four of these frame members have been constructed.

Frame members are permanently joined with flathead screws. Drill holes to accept the screws, this avoids the possibility of splitting the wood.

Use at least two flathead screws to fasten each of the four corners. The flathead screws should be set either flush with, or slightly below the surface of the wood.

Fabric: By stretching an open-mesh material over the frame, we complete the screen. Since this fabric must carry the stencil and allow the passage of ink, the selection should be considered critical.

SILK: Silk was the first fabric commonly used for making screens. This, as we mentioned earlier, accounts for the term, silk screen printing. However, because of its liabilities, it is at present probably the least desirable of available materials. Silk is available in rolls that range from 40″ to 80″ in width. It is produced in a variety of mesh counts varying from 54 threads per linear inch to 220 threads per linear inch. To understand mesh count, one must realize that most fabrics for screen printing are made with a taffeta weave—that is, threads cross under and over

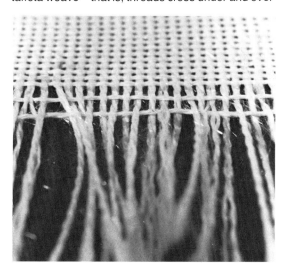

Taffeta weave—threads cross under and over at 90° angles.

each other at 90 degree angles. Fabrics are classified as to mesh count by counting the number of threads in a linear inch.

It is a fabric's normal characteristic that the fewer threads per linear inch, meaning the lower the mesh count, the more ink the fabric allows to be passed through it. Therefore, a 54 mesh count fabric will allow more ink to be deposited in one given impression than a 157 mesh count fabric. In part, this is also due to the fact that coarser mesh weaves are constructed of a heavier thread. Looking at illustration on pg. 8, you can see that the fabric of the coarser mesh weave count is thicker than the one of a finer mesh weave count.

An older system used for determining mesh for silk is known as mesh number. That system assigned a number followed by a series of x's which related to thread count per linear inch. The number of x's denotes the thickness of the thread used; x, xx, or xxx; xx silk is generally used for screen printing. An interesting aside to those who associate Pillsbury with x's—silk fabrics were originally developed for sifting flour and later adapted for printing.

As the mesh number goes up, the opening size and the percentage of open area goes down, thereby allowing less passage of ink.

The prime difficulty with an organic fabric like silk is its inability to retain dimensional stability. Because of its intense absorbent nature, silk has a strongly amorphous reaction to humidity and temperature factors. As a result, a very tightly stretched silk fabric screen can become very loose on damp days. This, in turn, can create extreme and sometimes insurmountable problems in making a multi-color print, where subsequent colors must fit colors printed earlier under different weather conditions.

Organdy fabrics are sometimes used in schools, where an inexpensive material is sought. Its characteristics make it even less suitable than silk for general usage and the problems generated usually offset any advantage in cost.

SYNTHETIC: We judge synthetic fabrics as the most acceptable type of support fabric.

The two synthetic materials in most common use today are nylon and polyester. While silk is an organic fabric made from the cocoon of the silkworm, both nylon and polyester are man-made.

As compared to silk, nylon is much more dimensionally stable, and polyester is almost completely unaffected by atmospheric humidity changes.

Coarse weave, fine weave. A fabric with fewer threads per linear inch, lower mesh count, allows more ink to be passed through it. Therefore, a 54-mesh count fabric allows more ink to be deposited than a 157-mesh count fabric. This is also due to the fact that coarser mesh weaves (above) are constructed of a heavier thread. You can see that the fabric of the coarser mesh weave is thicker than the one (below) of a finer mesh weave count. The smoothness of monofilament fabric is a result of its single thread (above right) construction. The twisted thread composition of each thread (below right) in a multifilament fabric gives it a characteristic coarseness or "tooth."

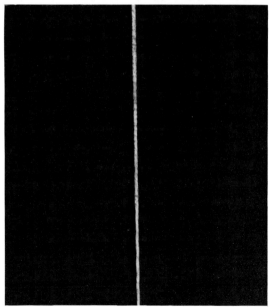

Polyester is considered the most stable of the fabrics we will discuss. (Although stainless steel and wire bronze fabrics are in use, their use is confined exclusively to commercial application in the electronics industries.)

Thread Construction: A fabric is composed of threads woven together. This means that the structure of the thread itself determines the texture and character of the fabric. There are basically two types of thread construction: 1) mono-filament, a single drawn thread where each thread consists of one element, 2) multi-filament, a single thread element which is formed by several smaller thread elements twisted together.

All silk fabrics are necessarily multi-filament. The individual threads of the cocoon weaving are much too fine to be used by themselves. Therefore, a number of threads are twisted together to form a single silk thread.

Nylon and polyester are each available as either mono-filament or multi-filament fabrics. There are assets inherent in the character of multi-filament fabrics. The surface of a multi-filament fabric has a tooth, or roughness, contributed by its twisted thread composition, which provides a marked advantage for attaching an indirect stencil (we will discuss indirect stencils later, see pg. 24) to the fabric. This "tooth" permits the stencil to adhere more readily. A disadvantage of multi-filament fabric is that the individual mesh openings, coarser because of their twisted thread nature, somewhat inhibit the passage of ink, and are slightly more difficult to clean after a printing operation. Mono-filament fabrics have the advantage of uniformity of individual mesh openings and the smoothness of the individual threads. This permits a more consistent and smooth flow of ink. The fabric tends to entrap less ink and is thereby easier to clean after a printing operation is completed. Its disadvantage is that it can be very difficult to attach an indirect-type stencil (either handmade or photographic) because of the smoothness of the fabric's surface.

For general use and to avoid complications, we suggest use of 12 xx (124 threads per linear inch) multi-filament polyester. As a multi-filament fabric, there will be more ease in adhering an indirect stencil. Also, we have found the 124 mesh count to be coarse enough to allow for adequate ink deposit and yet fine enough not to interfere with intricate details.

Attaching Fabric to Frame: There are a number of methods for attaching the fabric to the frame. The simplest type of attachment is called the cord and groove method. In this method, the underside of the frame has a groove that runs all around it.

To begin, the fabric is cut slightly larger than the outside dimension of the frame (allow 1″ on each of the four sides). The frame is placed on a firm flat surface, groove side up. The fabric is centered on the frame and loosely thumb-tacked at its four corners and sides. After doing this, a cord made specifically for this purpose (the cord bears a close resemblance to a clothesline), is placed on top of the fabric above the groove. Using a hammer, tap the cord lightly into the groove all around the frame, so that the fabric is lightly held in position by the cord. The thumb-tacks can now be removed from the four corners. Then, using a smooth piece of ⅞″ lattice wood or spline tool (available at most hardware stores, it is used to repair window screens) with a hammer, set the cord into its full depth. Rather than trying to accomplish this in one operation, it is best to work around the frame several times using light taps so that an evenly consistent stretch can be achieved. If a screen, at a later date, requires restretching, it is quite simple to remove the fabric by inserting a screwdriver under the cord, removing the cord and then restretching new fabric.

Attaching fabric to frame by stapling in a semi-permanent manner employs a staple gun and staples. Here again, the screen is placed on a firm, flat surface. The fabric is cut slightly larger than the outside frame dimensions (2″ on each of the four sides). The fabric is then attached by stapling in the sequence shown in the illustrations.

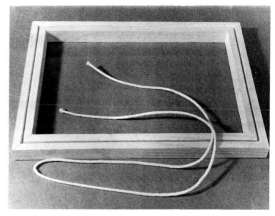

Attaching the fabric to the frame—cord and groove method. The underside of the frame has a groove which runs all around it.

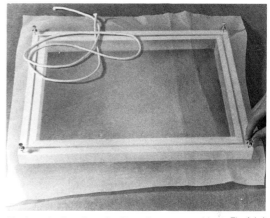

The frame is placed on a firm flat surface, groove side up. The fabric is centered on the frame and loosely tacked at its four corners and sides. The fabric is cut slightly larger than the outside dimension of the frame (allow 1″ on each of the four sides).

We have found it quite convenient when using the staple method to apply a product called staple-tape (available from most screen print suppliers). This is a strong cloth tape, available in rolls, that is cut to the length of each of the sides of the frame. The tape is placed on top of the fabric, centered on the wood and fabric. This means that the staples are inserted so

Using a hammer, tap the cord lightly into the groove all around the frame so that the fabric is lightly held in position by the cord. The tacks are removed after this is completed.

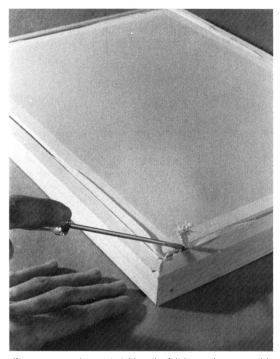

If a screen requires restretching, the fabric can be removed by inserting a screwdriver under the cord, and removing the cord.

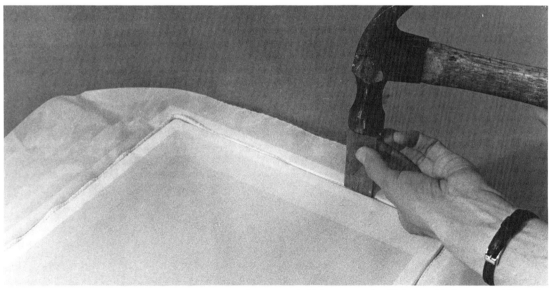

Using a ⅞" lattice wood wedge, set the cord into its full depth. Do not try to do this in one operation. Work around the frame several times using light taps for an evenly consistent stretch.

that they pass through the tape, the fabric and finally into the wooden frame below. The staple-tape prevents the staples from cutting the fabric unduly. It also makes it relatively simple to remove the staples when restretching is necessary. Since the tape is under the staples, the end of the tape can be grabbed with pliers and the tape and staples removed as a unit, rather than removing each staple individually.

When placing staples, insert them diagonally, rather than at a right angle, to the edge of the frame.

As you can see in the illustration, the fabric is stretched by working around the frame. We begin at the center of each frame member, inserting 3–4 staples, then move to the opposite side, pull the fabric taut and again insert 3–4 staples, move to one of the two unstapled sides, pull the fabric taut and insert 3–4 staples, move to the last side, pull the

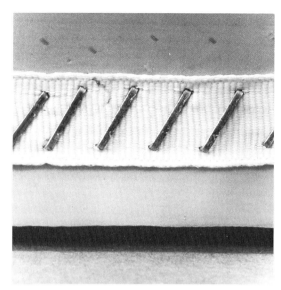

When placing staples, insert them diagonally rather than at a right angle to the edge of the frame.

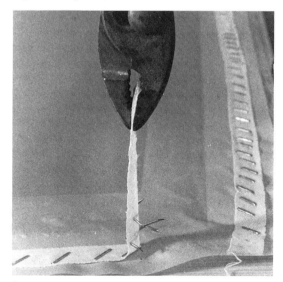

Staple Tape makes it relatively simple to remove staples when restretching. Since the tape is beneath the staples, the end of the tape can be grabbed with pliers, Tape and staples can be removed as a unit.

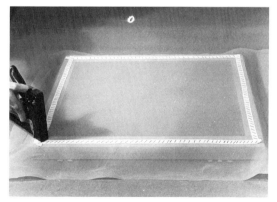

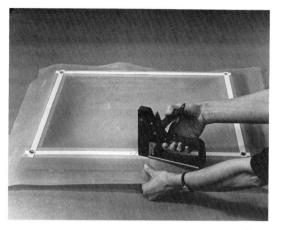

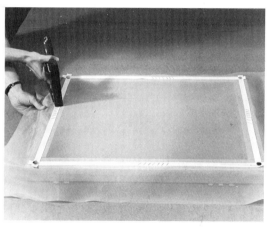

The fabric is stretched by working around the frame. Begin at the center of each frame member, insert three to four staples, move to the opposite side. Pull the fabric taut and insert three to four staples. Move to one of the two unstapled sides, pull the fabric taut and insert three to four staples. Move to the last side. Pull the fabric taut and again insert three to four staples. This procedure is continued, working toward the corners, moving around the frame inserting three to four staples in one side and then in its opposite. The object is a consistent tautness.

fabric taut and again insert 3–4 staples. This procedure is continued as begun, working toward the corners, moving around the frame, inserting 3–4 staples in one side and then in its opposite. The object is to achieve a consistent tautness. The fabric can be stretched with your fingers or with canvas-stretching pliers. Care, which comes with experience, must be taken not to stretch the fabric so tight that it rips. This particular possibility is more likely to occur when using canvas pliers since far more force is apt to be applied than with fingers.

SEALING: After the fabric has been stretched and before the screen is used, we suggest that the frame and interior edges where the frame and fabric meet, be sealed to facilitate the cleaning of the screen after each printing operation.

Cut strips of gummed paper tape that are slightly shorter than the interior dimensions of the frame. These strips should be folded into an "L" configuration running lengthwise; after which they are dampened and finally glued into position, smoothing out wrinkles and air bubbles.

When the gummed tape is thoroughly dry, a sealer, either a coat of shellac or preferably urethane varnish, is applied to *all* surfaces of the frame, including the gummed tape. When coating the tape, extend the sealer slightly beyond the edge of the tape into the exposed fabric (approximately ¼"). This will effectively seal all edges. We find it makes sense to apply three coats of sealer.

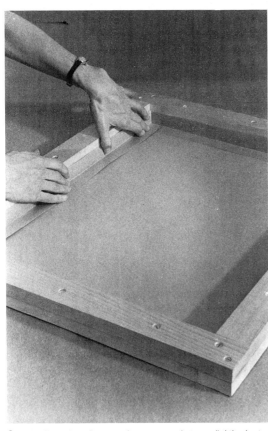

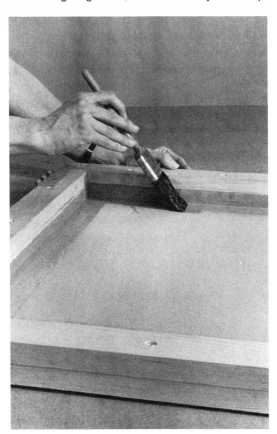

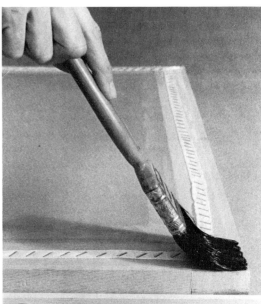

Sealing. Cut strips of gummed paper tape that are slightly shorter than the interior dimensions of the frame. These strips are folded into an "L" configuration running lengthwise. After they are dampened and glued into position, smooth out wrinkles and air bubbles.

When the gummed tape is thoroughly dry, a sealer—either a coat of shellac or urethane varnish is applied to all surfaces of the frame including the gummed tape. When coating the tape, extend the

sealer slightly beyond the edge of the tape into the exposed fabric—approximately ¼". This effectively seals all edges. We suggest you apply three coats of the sealer.

PRINTING BOARD

The other major component of the printing unit is a baseboard which holds the screen and forms the printing surface. The printing area must be flat and smooth since it supports the paper or other material being printed and carries the registration tabs for accurate stencil alignment. It must provide a convenient method for attaching and detaching the screen frame so that the screen can be easily cleaned, repaired and prepared.

Commercially, a special type of vacuum table or press serves this function. Less complex printing boards may also be purchased from most screen suppliers. We suggest building a simple printing board.

We recommend that you construct the printing board of ½″ thick exterior grade plywood. The plywood base should be six inches longer and wider than the largest screen which is to be used on it. A hinge bar can then be made with a piece of lumber of the same thickness and width as that used for the screen frames. This strip is cut to the same length as the width of the plywood base, and is attached to the back of the plywood base by drilling a hole through the hinge bar itself and through the plywood base at each end of the hinge bar. A carriage bolt is inserted in each of the drilled holes so that it passes through the hinge bar and through the plywood base, and a washer and nut is attached to each of the carriage bolts to secure the hinge bar to the base.

Bolts are used rather than nails or screws because they permit the hinge bar to be raised by placing pieces of cardboard between the base and the hinge bar. The importance of this flexibility will be apparent when we cover the actual printing operation.

Hinges are attached to the hinge bar in the following way: The screen to be used is placed on the printing board so that one of its sides is in contact with the hinge bar. Loose-pin hinges are fastened to the hinge bar and to the screen frame by drilling holes and attaching the hinges as illustrated.

The term, loose-pin hinge derives from the fact that the pin which holds the two sides of the hinge to-

The printing board can be constructed of ½″-thick exterior grade plywood, which should be 6″ longer and wider than the widest screen which will be used on it.

gether can be withdrawn so that the two parts separate. This allows a screen to be removed from the printing board by simply pulling the hinge pins out.

The hinge elements remain attached to the frame and the hinge bar. Thus a screen can be installed for future printing or stencil operations by slipping it back into position with the hinge bar and then reinserting the hinge pins. When buying hinges, be sure to purchase several sets by the same manufacturer, of the exact same design. This will insure interchangeability. Hinge elements can be attached to any number of screens, so that they match those on the hinge bar. This guarantees that many screens can be mounted to the same hinge bar.

Loose-pin hinges are made with one half of the hinge as a two-loop element and the other a three-loop element.

A hinge bar can be made with a piece of lumber of the same thickness and width as that used for the screen frames. The strip is cut to the same length as the width of the plywood base. It is attached to the back of the plywood base by drilling a hole through the hinge bar and through the plywood base at each end of the hinge bar.

A carriage bolt is inserted in each drilled hole so that it passes through the hinge bar and the plywood base. A washer and nut are attached to each carriage bolt to secure the hinge bar to the base.

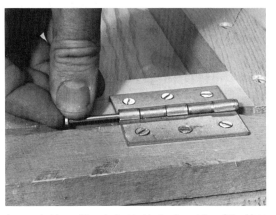

Loose pin hinge. The pin that holds the two sides of the hinge together can be withdrawn so that the two parts separate. This allows the screen to be removed from the printing board by simply pulling the hinge pins out.

The hinge elements remain attached to the frame and the hinge bar. Thus, a screen can be installed by slipping it back into position with the hinge bar and reinserting the hinge pins.

Hinges are attached to the hinge bar—the screen is placed on the printing board against the hinge bar. Loose pin hinges are fastened to the hinge bar and to the screen frame by drilling holes and attaching the hinges as shown.

Loose pin hinges are made with one-half of the hinge as a two-loop element and the other, a three-loop element.

Using the two halves of a single-hinge set, the two-loop element is attached to one end of the hinge bar and the three-loop element is attached to the other end of the hinge bar. This allows screen attachment to be made by affixing the two parts of an identical hinge set to the screen frame. The three-loop element unites with the two-loop element on the bar and is secured by inserting the hinge pin. The two-loop element is joined to the three-loop element at the other end of the hinge bar and is united with a pin. This insures alignment of the hinges and provides an economy—only one hinge set will be necessary for attaching any new screen.

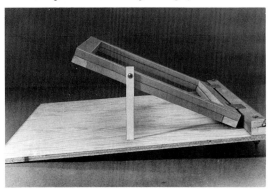

A kick-leg can easily be made once a screen is mounted on the base in the printing position. A point is marked on the side of the screen frame ⅓ back. The screen is raised on an angle of approximately 30° to the base—the vertical distance between the mark on the angled frame and the baseboard is measured. A strip of ⅞" lattice wood is cut 1" longer than this measured distance. A hole is drilled, centered about 1" from the end of the wooden strip. A wood screw is selected that can penetrate the strip and enter approximately ⅔ of the frame's depth. The hole drilled through the (wood strip) kick-leg, should enable the kick-leg to swing freely around the screw. As you see, when the screen is raised, the kick-leg assumes a vertical position and holds the screen in a raised position.

To lower the screen, the kick-leg is simply pushed back or forward and the screen brought down.

Using the two halves of a single hinge set, attach the two-loop element to one end and the three-loop element to the other end of the hinge bar. This allows screen attachment to be made by affixing the two parts of an identical hinge set to the screen frame. The three-loop element is screwed on to the frame, so that when the screen is positioned in contact with the hinge bar, that three-loop element unites with the two-loop element on the bar, and is secured by inserting the hinge pin. The same procedure is followed to hinge the two-loop element to the frame and join it to the three-loop element at the other end of the hinge bar.

Following these directions will insure the alignment of the hinges as well as provide an economy, since only one hinge set will be necessary to attach a new screen.

We now have a screen attached to a rigid base so that it may be raised and lowered from the same position relative to the base. We will need a device to maintain the screen in a raised position. These devices, called kick-legs, are available from screen printing suppliers. However, a kick-leg can easily be made once a screen is mounted on the base in the printing position. A point is marked on the right hand side of the screen frame about ⅓ back from the front edge. The screen is raised so that it is at an angle of approximately 30 degrees to the base, and the vertical distance between the mark on the angled frame and the baseboard is measured. A strip of light wood (such as 1 x 2) is cut about 1" longer than this measured distance. A hole is drilled, centered about 1" from the end of this wooden strip, and a wood screw is selected that will penetrate the strip and enter the frame. The screw should be long enough to pass into approximately ⅔ of the frame's depth. The hole drilled through the wood strip, or kick-leg, should be sufficiently wide in diameter to enable the kick-leg to swing freely around the screw. As you see, when the screen is raised, the kick-leg assumes a vertical position and holds the screen in a raised position. To lower the screen, the kick-leg is simply pushed back and the screen lowered.

THE SQUEEGEE

The squeegee is the tool which applies the ink. It must pull ink across the screen and force it through the open stencil areas on to the paper or other material being printed. The squeegee consists of a blade mounted in a handle. Blades are either plastic or rubber. Some squeegees have plastic or metal handles, but most have wooden handles. Squeegees are available in different sizes. The length of the squeegee will be determined by the format size. Squeegees are sold at most art stores. A squeegee cut to size with a choice of handles can be purchased from screen supply houses.

There are two basic squeegee handles, the classic and the eastern style. The classic handle is most frequently used. It is a piece of wood shaped so that it may be comfortably grasped. It should allow the fingers to be straightened out without extending beyond the lip of the blade socket. The eastern style squeegee features a vertical wooden handle attached to the center of the wooden strip that holds the blade. It is grasped with one hand, and pushed rather than pulled like the classic style squeegee. Both types work well. Our personal preference is for the classic style squeegee.

INKS, SOLVENTS & STOCKS
Inks

Printing inks are composed of three elements, the pigment, the varnish or binder and the solvent. The pigment is the component which determines the color. Pigments can be either naturally occurring materials, such as the earth colors (sienna, ochre) or they can be man-made. The varnish binds the individual pigment particles together to form a film when dry. The solvent reduces the viscosity of the pigment/varnish combination to a printable consistency.

Most inks are available as flat, matte finishes, or with some degree of gloss. The finish, flat or gloss, results from the type and amount of varnish used.
POSTER INKS: The most generally used screen printing ink is "poster" ink. It is available with either a

Classic style handle squeegee.

Eastern style handle squeegee.

flat or a gloss finish, and the two can be mixed to form a semi-gloss finish. These inks are soluble in mineral spirits. Their drying time is approximately 30–45 minutes. Poster inks dry by the evaporation of their solvent content. Some manufacturers are now producing poster inks that are water soluble. This is a great convenience because *no* solvents other than water are needed for clean-up. When using water soluble inks, be sure you read and follow the manufacturer's instructions. These inks cannot be used with water soluble stencil, such as block-out glue or photographic emulsions. One notable exception here is the Hunt/Speedball System. All of their stencils, direct, resist or photographic, can be used in combination with water soluble, solvent, acrylic or textile inks.

FLUORESCENT INKS: These inks are composed of specially formulated pigments which have very high light reflectivity—they virtually appear to be glowing. One word of caution: these inks have a fugitive nature and will fade or actually vanish if exposed to strong sunlight.

ENAMEL INKS: Enamel inks are formulated with a different varnish than poster inks. While poster inks dry by evaporation and in a relatively short time, enamels dry by internal chemical reaction with the available air (oxidation) rather slowly. Drying time can run anywhere between six to twenty-four hours. The ink forms a very tough, durable surface and has the highest gloss level of the commonly available inks.

Drying. String a rope or clothesline between two points.

Bulldog clips which hold the prints while drying.

TEXTILE INKS: This important ink category is available soluble in water or in mineral spirits. Some textile inks will air dry but most require exposure to a baking cycle of 275–375 degrees to fully set the ink and make it washable.

In addition to the inks mentioned, there are many specialty inks available for special applications. These include lacquer, epoxy and plastic inks, as well as metallic inks such as gold and silver.

Solvents: We will deal with three solvents: *water,* as a solvent for water soluble inks and as a solvent to remove water soluble block-outs and films; *mineral spirits*, as a solvent and wash-up material for poster inks or enamels; and *acetone*, a strong solvent to be used only when ink has been allowed to dry in a screen and cannot be removed with mineral spirits.

Stock: Screen printing's great versatility is that it can be applied to virtually any type of surface. It can be used to print on flat surfaces such as paper, cardboard (posters, etc.), or irregular surfaces such as bottles, metal parts, etc.

PAPER: As a paper culture, we are richly endowed with an almost limitless selection of textures, colors, weights and sizes of paper. Paper is available from stationers, paper suppliers and art supply stores. The selection should be individual, or course. However, we do suggest that when doing fine arts printing, the paper used be a serious consideration. The highest quality paper is made of 100% cotton fiber and has a neutral PH factor. Neutral PH means the paper is neither acidic nor caustic. Therefore, its color will remain stable over a long time span and it will not change the colors that have been printed on it. The new selected series of *Bienfang* Papers and Boards are excellent.

CARDBOARD: Again, the abundant possibilities require you to look around. Most art supply stores carry a wide selection of colors, sizes and weights.

TEXTILES: One can quite easily screen print on garments such as "T" shirts, that are ready to wear or on fabric that will be made into items after printing. Prior to printing on any fabric, be certain that sizing has been removed to assure proper adhesion of the textile inks. Also, be aware of heat setting requirements if the fabric is to be washed after printing.

MISCELLANEOUS MATERIALS: Screen printing is also employed to print on a vast variety of other materials; to mention a few—leather, wood, glass, plastics, metal, ceramics.

DRYING

Most of the inks you will be involved with dry within 30–45 minutes. This means there must be a way of separating the printed images until they have dried and can be stacked. The simplest method, of course, is to spread the sheets out on any convenient flat surface. This will work if the number being printed is small. Another solution is to string a rope between two points and with wooden clothespins or Bulldog clips, hang the prints for drying. The clothespins should be drilled and strung on the line.

There are commercial racks made especially for drying prints. Their cost is prohibitive unless there is sufficient work to justify such expensive equipment.

Commercially built drying racks.

CHAPTER 3

Screen printing is more than a process for graphic reproduction. It provides a flexible means for transforming ideas into visual reality. Familiarity with the medium will influence the visual form the idea takes.

How an idea for a print emerges is a personal matter between the artist and the medium. A full color layout can be worked out and each color separated for stencil preparation. In contrast, a simple sketch or photograph can serve as a guide. In fact, working spontaneously with no guide at all is also viable. A combination of the various methods is another alternative. Whatever means accommodate making the idea visually tangible, stencils will have to be prepared. The stencils carry the image from concept to final printed state.

THE STENCIL

The stencil functions as a mask with open areas which allow ink to pass through to the paper or other material beneath it. The covered areas act as a mask which block the flow of ink. There are four basic screen printing stencil types—hand-cut, block-out, tusche resist and photographic. In this chapter, we will describe the principles and methods for making each type of stencil. Later, in Chapter VI, we will illustrate and demonstrate the incorporation of each of the stencil types in the production of a screen print, specifically detailing procedures and materials.

Hand-Cut Stencil: This stencil involves cutting a mask in paper or in a special film stencil made specifically as a separate element for screen printing. After it has been cut, the hand-cut stencil is attached to the screen.

Hand-Cut Paper Stencil: The hand-cut paper stencil is the simplest form of stencil. The materials required can be readily obtained. To make this stencil, we suggest using a heavy tracing paper, which is

Hand-cut paper stencil. Heavy tracing paper placed over artwork so that the image can be traced directly.
After the image has been traced, the paper is removed to a sheet of cardboard or comparable surface for cutting. The best tool for this cutting is an Exacto-type knife with a pointed blade. The blade is razor sharp to prevent the paper from ripping or tearing. You cut the image, discarding pieces that represent areas you wish to print. What is retained as the mask are the areas that will not be printed.

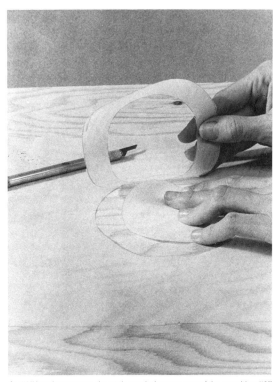

An "0" has been traced; cut through the paper and the resulting "0" has been discarded to leave a stencil of an "0".

sufficiently transparent to be placed over art work so that the image can be traced directly. After the image has been traced on to the paper, the paper is removed from the art work and placed on a sheet of cardboard or comparable surface, for cutting. The best tool for this cutting is an "Exacto"-type knife with a pointed blade. It is important that the blade be razor sharp to prevent the paper from ripping and tearing. Let's remember that you cut the image by discarding pieces that represent the areas you want to print or, in other words, what is retained as the mask, are the areas that do not print.

In the illustration, it is evident that an "O" has been traced on the paper mask, cut through the paper mask, and the resulting "O" has been discarded to leave a stencil of an "O". You can also see that the outside of the stencil representing the outside of the "O" is in no way connected to the inside of the "O". To complete the mounting of the stencil to the screen fabric, we will tape the paper to the underside of the screen with masking tape. No problem will arise with attachment of the outside of the "O" because the outside edges of the mask can be taped directly to the screen fabric. However, there is no way to tape the inside of the "O" to the fabric without interfering with the passage of the ink. To solve this problem, we place a few dabs of a water soluble glue, such as Elmer's or LePage's on the center of the "O", then lightly place the center of the "O" in contact with the screen and allow the glue to dry.

The outside of the stencil, representing the outside of the "0" is in no way connected to the inside of the "0". To complete the mounting of the stencil to the screen fabric, tape the paper to the underside of the screen with masking tape.

There is no way to tape the inside of the "0" to the fabric without interfering with the passage of ink. Place a few dabs of water soluble glue on the center of the "0", then place the center of the "0" in contact with the screen, allow the glue to dry. Note: water soluble glue can be used only if the ink being printed is not water soluble. If water soluble ink is used, rubber cement can be used.

Hand-cut film stencil is composed of a thin lacquer (or water based) film, bonded to a transparent plastic backing sheet.

Water soluble glue can be used only if the ink being printed through the stencil is *not* water soluble. Obviously, since water soluble ink and water soluble glue are soluble in the same solvent (water), the ink would quickly dissolve the glue and allow the center of the "0" to move. If a water soluble ink is to be used, rubber cement can be applied to attach the center of the "0" or any free form within a design. Quite often, if only a small number of pieces are to be printed, the paper-stencil can be placed with the free element (such as the center of "0") in position under the screen, the screen let down on top of the paper stencil and ink passed across it. The adhesive nature of the ink will hold the elements in place for a very limited number of impressions.

Hand-Cut Film Stencil: The other hand-cut stencil is made with a commercially prepared film. This film is composed of a very thin film lightly bonded to a transparent plastic backing sheet. Here too, let's talk about the "0" used in the hand-cut paper stencil method. The transparent film is placed over a drawing of the "0". A small Exacto knife with a very sharp pointed blade cuts the interior and exterior outlines of the "0". The area representing the "0" is peeled away revealing the defined outside and inside areas. Since the inside of the "0" is still bound to the clear plastic backing sheet, there is no problem with the inside of the "0" moving. The films of this type are divided into two categories, according to the solvent that dissolves the film. One group is soluble in water,

the other soluble in a strong solvent such as lacquer thinner. After the stencil is cut and the printing area peeled away and discarded, the film is placed on a slightly raised pad made of cardboard or other smooth material. The clean screen is placed directly on top of the pad, fabric side down and weights placed on the frame. The purpose of the pad is to insure good contact between the stencil film and the clean fabric. The raised pad should be smaller than the inside dimensions of the frame so that the fabric and not the frame rests on it. After this is done, proper solvent or adhering liquid for the stencil film is applied to the inside surface of the screen fabric so that it penetrates the fabric and softens the stencil film below. This allows the fabric to permeate the softened stencil film so that after the solvent evaporates, a bond is formed between the fabric and the stencil film. The method we find most successful for applying the solvent employs two pads made of soft absorbent paper towels. One of these pads is thoroughly saturated with the proper solvent for the stencil film and used to thoroughly dampen an area of the film about 10″ square. It is important to use enough solvent to wet the stencil film. However, caution should be exercised in not applying too much solvent with too much pressure. After this, the dry pad of paper towels is immediately used to blot up any excess fluid. A gentle pressure is applied to the dry pad to lightly force the fabric into the softened stencil film. This procedure is not intended for large

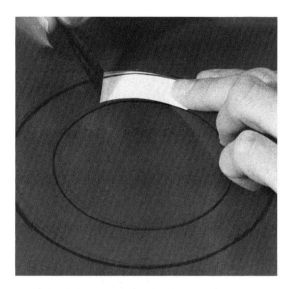

areas. Caution dictates working on small areas at a time. When the entire stencil has been adhered to the fabric in this manner, place a small electric fan so that a flow of air is directed across the fabric—this removes residual solvent. The weighted screen remains on the raised pad during the fanning. When the screen is thoroughly dry, it is removed from the weighted pad and placed on a flat surface with the film side up. Should there be an open border area on the screen fabric between the stencil film and the inside of the wooden frame, screen filler should be applied to this opening. This will prevent ink from penetrating. A screen filler material soluble in the same solvent as the hand-cut stencil film, water or lacquer thinner must be used. A fan should be placed near the screen to dry the stencil filler. When dry, the clear plastic backing of the hand-cut stencil film can be gently lifted at a corner and peeled away, leaving the film attached to the screen fabric. At this point, a second coat of screen filler is applied, which slightly overlaps the outside edge of the stencil film and the inside edge of the wooden screen frame. A small amount of the stencil filler is poured on the fabric and then with a stiff piece of cardboard, squeegeed across the desired area. Care must be taken that any areas to be printed are *not* covered with stencil filler.

The solvents for these films are either water or lacquer thinner type solvents. A water soluble type stencil film cannot be used with a water soluble ink; a lacquer soluble type stencil film cannot be used with a lacquer type ink. Every manufacturer of hand-cut stencil films packs instructions with the product. We strongly urge that these instructions be carefully read and followed.

To return for a moment to the cutting operation performed on the stencil film, we would like to comment on two points. First, we stressed that in the cutting operation, the blade used be pointed and very sharp. Because the film is a two-layer material, film and plastic backing, it is essential that you try to cut through the film side without cutting into or embossing the plastic backing. The reason for this is that should the plastic film backing be deeply cut or

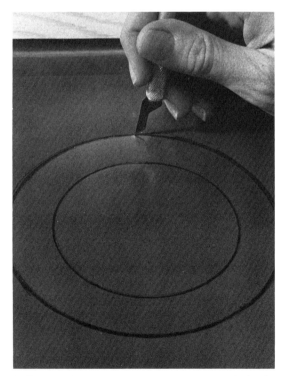

An Exacto knife with a very sharp pointed blade cuts the interior and exterior outlines of the "0".

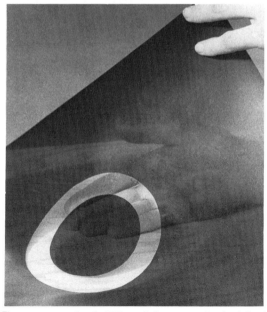

The area representing the "0" is peeled away revealing the defined outside and inside areas. The inside of the "0" is still bound to the plastic backing sheet.

scored, this cut or score will become a reservoir for adhering solvents and will overdissolve or "burn" the edges of the cut image, resulting in a soft or ragged edge. Since one of the prime virtues of a hand-cut stencil is its sharp clean edge, it is therefore essential that this caution be well observed. The second comment is about "overcutting". This point can be illustrated by picturing two intersecting lines cut in the film to form a 90 degree angle. The two lines should be extended slightly beyond their intersection to insure that the cuts actually meet. As a result, when the film is peeled away, there will be no tendency for the film to tear at such intersections. When the film is attached to the screen fabric with solvent, the overcut will seal itself.

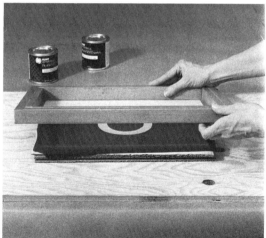

The clean screen is placed directly on top of a raised pad made of cardboard. The raised pad should be smaller than the inside dimensions of the frame so that the fabric and not the frame rests on it.

After the screen is placed on the raised cardboard, adhering liquid for the stencil film is applied to the screen fabric so that it penetrates the fabric and softens the stencil film. The fabric permeates the softened stencil film so that after the solvent evaporates, a bond is formed between the fabric and the stencil film. Two pads of soft absorbent paper towels are used. One pad is thoroughly saturated with the proper solvent for the stencil film and is used to dampen an area of film about 10" sq. The second, dry pad of paper towels blots up excess fluid. A gentle pressure is applied to the dry pad to lightly force the fabric into the softened stencil film. Work on small areas at a time until the entire stencil is adhered to the fabric in this manner.

Should there be an open border area between the stencil film and the wooden frame, a screen filler is applied to it. A screen filler soluble in the same solvent as the hand-cut stencil film, must be used.

Direct Block-Out Stencil: In hand-cut stencils we cut away the areas which are to be printed. Therefore, we consider it a positive working system as opposed to the direct block-out method which fills in the areas *not* being printed, and is therefore classified as a negative stencil.

The direct block-out stencil also differs from the hand-cut stencil in that all operations are performed directly on the fabric itself. This is accommodated by placing a clean screen directly over the art work or layout desired. The image to be printed is traced with a soft pencil onto the screen fabric. After tracing, the screen is removed from the art work and placed on small blocks so that it does not touch the surface below it. A suitable block-out material is used, with appropriate size brushes, to fill in all areas *not* to be printed. When all the "no print" areas on the screen fabric have been filled in, the screen is dried and the stencil is ready to print. This method lends itself to soft, sketchy edges and shapes.

Block-outs fall into basic categories: water soluble and those soluble in strong solvents like lacquer thinner and acetone. Again, we stress that a water soluble block-out or screen filler *not* be used if the ink to be used is water soluble. There are exceptions to this such as the Hunt/Speedball Screen Filler which is removed with hot water, but can be used with either water soluble or water resist inks. The same premise holds true for a lacquer soluble screen filler—it should not be used with a lacquer ink. Sometimes, more than one coat of screen filler may be needed to completely close the mesh. Decide this, by holding the block-out screen up to a light source or window, looking for any pin holes or spaces in areas that are intended to be closed. If there are such openings, a brush is used to apply additional screen filler to block them.

Tusche-Resist Stencil: With this type of stencil, we again work directly on the screen fabric. To make a tusche-resist stencil, again, the clean screen is placed over the art work and the image traced on the screen fabric with a soft pencil, after which the screen is removed and placed on small blocks so it does not touch the surface below. An oily substance called tusche is then used with appropriate size brushes to paint in the areas that *are* to be printed. When the tusche is dry—once more, a fan will expedite drying. A water soluble glue is squeegeed with a stiff piece of cardboard across the entire inside of the screen fabric. The glue coating is dried by fan. When thoroughly dry, the screen is placed flat on a pad made of several layers of newspaper, and mineral spirits or turpentine are poured into the screen to thoroughly saturate it. Since the glue that has been squeegeed on is water soluble, the mineral spirits or turpentine will not affect it. However, with a little light rubbing, the solvent dissolves the tusche which is soluble in it. When the tusche has been completely removed, it will leave open areas which allow for passage of ink, while the water soluble glue will act as a screen filler. Tusche is available in prepared liquid form from screen print suppliers. It is also produced in semi-hard pencil or crayon form that can be used instead of brushing. This pencil or crayon form of tusche can assist in creating textures by placing a rough surface under the screen fabric and rubbing across the top of the screen with the pencil or crayon tusche, you can pick up the texture of the surface beneath. The glue used most frequently is LePage's Liquid Hide glue. We suggest you dilute this glue in half and half pro-

The stencil filler is squeegeed with a piece of cardboard. Care must be taken that any areas to be printed are not covered with stencil filler.

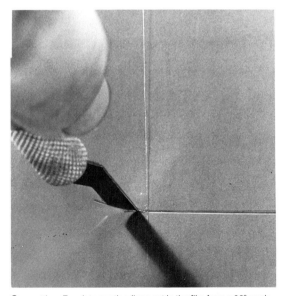

Overcutting. Two intersecting lines cut in the film form a 90° angle. The two lines should be extended slightly beyond their intersection to insure that the cuts actually meet. When the film is peeled away it will not tear at such intersections. When the film is adhered to the screen fabric with solvent, the overcut will seal itself.

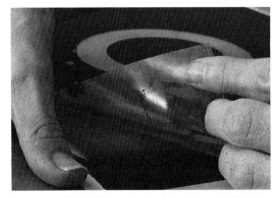

When screen filler is dry, the clear plastic backing can be lifted at a corner and peeled away.

Block-out stencil. A clean screen is placed directly over artwork. The image is traced with a soft pencil onto the screen fabric.

portion with plain water and then add ten drops of glycerine per cup to this half and half mixture. The glycerine helps the glue remain flexible so that it will not crack during the printing operation.

Hunt/Speedball has developed a method that is essentially the tusche-resist system, but does not require the use of any solvents except water. In this method, a water soluble liquid material called Drawing Fluid is used instead of tusche. After the drawing has been made on the clean screen with the Drawing Fluid, the newly drawn image is allowed to dry. A flow of air from a fan will accomplish the drying in about ½ hour. Hunt/Speedball Screen Filler made specifically for this purpose, is then squeegeed over the Drawing Fluid in the same way as the glue in the tusche-resist method. The screen is left to dry overnight. When thoroughly dry, the screen is washed in cold water which will remove the Drawing Fluid. A stiff bristle scrub brush used with cold water will assist in removing the Drawing Fluid. You are now equipped with a stencil which is ready for printing. After the screen has been used for printing and all ink and solvent has been removed, the Screen Filler can be removed with hot water and a detergent solution made with a household product such as Spic 'n Span. Again, a stiff nylon bristle brush should be used to scrub the screen clean.

After tracing, the screen is removed and placed on small blocks so that it does not touch the surface below it.

A suitable block-out material is used with appropriate sized brushes, to fill in all areas not to be printed. When all "no print" areas have been filled in, the screen is dried. Sometimes, more than one coat of screen filler is needed to completely close the mesh. Decide this by holding screen up to a light source, looking for pin holes or spaces in areas that should be closed.

Tusche-resist stencil.

The screen is placed on small blocks so it does not touch the surface below. Tusche is used with appropriate sized brushes to paint in the areas that are to be printed. Hunt/Speedball Drawing Fluid can be substituted for tusche in Hunt's system.

Tusche is available in semi-hard pencil or crayon form as well as liquid form. To create textures, a rough surface, in this case, a rubber stamp—FIRST CLASS—has been placed under the screen fabric. By rubbing across the top of the screen fabric with the crayon tusche, the texture of the surface has been picked up.

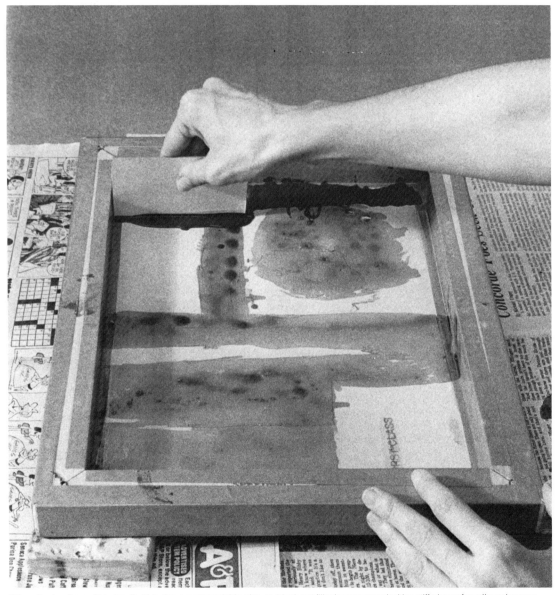

When the tusche or Drawing Fluid is dry, a water soluble glue or block-out filler is squeegeed with a stiff piece of cardboard across the entire screen fabric and left to dry.

Photographic Stencil: The most versatile and, in our opinion, most utilitarian stencil is the photographic type. This stencil process depends on the ability of certain bichromate or diazo materials to be hardened by light. There are three methods for making a photographic stencil; they are—the indirect, the direct, and the direct/indirect.

Indirect Photographic Stencil: This photographic stencil employs a film that comes in sheet or roll form. The most popular indirect film is composed of a gelatin-like substance coated on a clear plastic backing. To make an indirect photographic stencil, this film is cut slightly larger than the size of the image to be placed on it. The film and the positive are placed in contact with each other, usually in a vacuum contact frame or under weighted glass, and exposed to an appropriate light source.

The "positive" referred to can be an actual photographic image on clear base film or it can be made by drawing or painting directly on a clear film with an opaque liquid like photographer's opaque or black india ink. The areas of density in either the photographic or hand prepared positive will block light from reaching areas of the stencil film that they cover. When the stencil film and positive are sandwiched together and placed under pressure, the light hardens, or makes insoluble in water, any of the areas of the stencil film with which it comes in contact. After the exposure to light is made, the film and positive are removed and the film is treated in a sensitizer bath, a solution of peroxide and water. The sensitizers are available as a two-part powder system to be mixed with a specific amount of water to make a peroxide solution of the correct percentage. Read the manufacturer's instructions carefully. After sensitizing, the next step is to gently wash the film side (not plastic-backing side) with a gentle flow of warm water. A hand sprayer hose like the kind that fits over a household faucet head is adequate for this washout. The washed out image, still wet, is placed on a pad of newspaper or cardboard about ¼" thick, with the plastic side down. The clean screen is positioned about it and lowered gently into the damp emulsion. The frame is weighted and newsprint (or inexpensive paper) is used to gently blot up excess moisture. This blotting also serves to press the screen fabric into the soft emulsion. A stream of air from a fan directed on the image will thoroughly dry it. When the screen/stencil combination is dry, the screen can be removed from the weighted position and placed on a flat surface with the fabric side of the frame up. A water soluble screen filler is applied to block areas of the screen fabric, including pin holes that should not be printed.

Direct Photographic Stencil: In Chapter VI, we will be printing this photographic type of stencil. We consider it the simplest and the most dependable stencil. A thick syrupy liquid emulsion is used to coat the clean screen fabric directly. The coated screen is dried. Again, a positive, either photographic or hand-drawn, is placed on the dried emulsion and exposed to a light source. After exposure, the screen is washed with a flow of warm water which removes the parts of the stencil that have been masked by the positive. The screen is dried and any area, space, or pin hole not intended for printing is filled in with water soluble screen filler. When the screen filler is dry, the stencil is ready for printing.

Direct photographic emulsions are two-part mixtures. One part is the emulsion itself, which is not light sensitive until the second part, the sensitizer, is added. There are two direct-method emulsion types. One is made with a diazo sensitizer and the other with a bichromate sensitizer. The bichromate sensitized emulsion is designed for quick exposure and excellent solvent resistance. It can be used with most any kind of screen printing ink. Because of its high viscosity and fast drying qualities, bichromate emulsions are easily applied to all fabrics. Bichromates can lose their effectiveness within a 4-6 hour period. Diazo sensitized emulsions have a longer life. Diazo mixture can be stored up to 3 months at room temperature and if refrigerated—up to 6 months. Diazo emulsions, however, require approximately 2-3

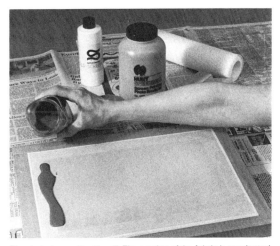

Direct photographic stencil. The coating of the fabric is conducted by placing the clean screen on blocks resting on a flat surface, with fabric side up. A small amount of emulsion is poured across one end of the screen.

times longer exposure time than bichromate emulsions. They are also more difficult to remove.

The coating of the fabric is carried out by placing the clean screen on blocks resting on a flat surface, fabric side up. A small amount of emulsion is poured across one end of the screen and a squeegee or stiff piece of cardboard of appropriate length is used to pull the emulsion smoothly across the screen. The emulsion is squeegeed back across the screen in the opposite direction, thus giving the screen two coats. Any excess emulsion is scooped up from the screen with small pieces of cardboard and placed back in the container of sensitized emulsion. Next, the screen is turned over with the frame side up. The blocks supporting the screen are important because the coated screen must *not* rest on the surface below it. The coating operation is carried out on the inside screen fabric in the same manner just described. After this application has been completed and any excess emulsion removed, the screen is placed in a dark or low light level area for drying. A closet or similarly dark area is appropriate. Wherever possible, dry the screen in a horizontal position—fabric side down.

A squeegee or stiff piece of cardboard is used to pull the emulsion smoothly across the screen. The emulsion is squeegeed back across the screen in the opposite direction, thus giving the screen two coats. The blocks supporting the screen are essential so that the coated screen does not rest on the surface below it.

The screen is turned over. The coating operation is carried out on the inside screen fabric in the same manner.

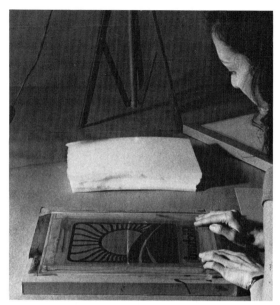

Mounting photographic positive. When the emulsion is dry, the positive can be mounted. A foam rubber pad approximately 2" thick and an inch or two smaller than the inside of the screen is placed on a flat surface. The screen is placed in the center of the foam rubber pad fabric side up. The only part of the screen resting on the foam rubber should be the fabric.

The positive is placed directly on the photographic emulsion. The positive must be placed directly so that the image, as viewed, reads backwards. Notice the name Richard in the photograph.

Mounting Photographic Positive: When the emulsion is dry, the screen is ready to be exposed. The first method for mounting the positive to the dry emulsion that we will describe uses a foam rubber pad approximately two inches thick and an inch or two smaller in both directions than the inside dimensions of the screen frame being used. This foam rubber pad is placed on a flat surface, then the screen is placed in the center of the foam rubber pad, fabric side up. The only part of the screen resting on the foam rubber should be the fabric. The positive is placed directly on the photographic emulsion. The positive must be placed so that the image as viewed reads backwards. A piece of glass is placed on top of the positive, to insure intimate contact between the positive and the emulsion.

When contact is achieved, the emulsion is ready for exposure to a light source.

We have experienced much success with a second, simpler method than the one just described for positive/emulsion contact. In this procedure, the fabric side of the emulsion coated screen is sprayed with a light coat of contact cement (any of the several types available for mounting photographs will work). This cement spray coating is dried for three to four minutes, after which the positive, again reading backwards, is placed in position on the emulsion and gently rubbed down, removing any air bubbles.

The screen is now ready to be exposed. After exposure, the positive is peeled away from the emulsion and the screen is washed out in the usual manner. When the screen has dried, areas and pin holes not being printed are blocked in with a water soluble screen filler and allowed to dry. Prior to printing, the underside of the screen that was sprayed with the contact cement is wiped down with mineral spirits. This removes any tackiness remaining from the spray adhesive.

Direct/Indirect Photographic Stencil: The most recently popularized photographic stencil is the direct/indirect stencil. This method is basically a combination of indirect photo film, available in a dry form, as sheets or rolls and direct emulsion. A piece of indirect photo film, larger than the image to be made is cut and placed with the emulsion side up on a larger sheet of clean newsprint or paper. The clean screen is then placed with the fabric side down on top of the piece of film. A sensitized direct emulsion is prepared. A bead of this emulsion mixture is poured along one end of the screen fabric and squeegeed across the cut film below. This operation permits the wet photo emulsion to penetrate the screen fabric and attaches the indirect photo-film to the screen fabric. The screen/emulsion/film combination is dried in a horizontal position with a fan. When the emulsion is thoroughly dry, the backing sheet is peeled away. All procedures following this are the same as those described for direct emulsion screens. The principal advantage of the direct/indirect photo stencil is its ability to create an even, pre-determined thickness. *NOTE:* All the photographic stencils we have discussed are water soluble and should not be used with water soluble inks. There are exceptions, such as the Hunt/Speedball Photo System. This unique system can be used with water soluble inks, solvent inks, acrylic inks or textile inks. This can be advantageous, since mineral spirits or other stronger solvents are not needed for wash up. Other manufacturers make specific photographic emulsions for use with water soluble based systems as well as products that can be coated onto the completed stencil to allow the use of water soluble inks. Again, read and follow instructions supplied by the manufacturer.

Light Source for Exposure: The emulsion used for most stencil processes is primarily sensitive to the blue or ultra-violet end of the light spectrum. Commercially, most exposures are made with white flame carbon arc lamps or pulsed xenon lamps. However, these units are quite expensive. We find that a 150 watt household bulb or a B.B.A. #1 photo-flood bulb will work very well. It is necessary to remember that the dry screen is light sensitive and any handling prior to exposure should take place in a reduced light area—it does not have to be totally dark—one could safely work in an area where a 75 watt bulb is at least six feet from the coated screen.

Exposure is very important. It is a result of the distance between the light source and the positive as well as the duration of exposure. The correct distance of the light source is determined by measuring the diagonal distance of the positive image to be used. The light source should never be placed closer than this diagonal measurement. Since the photoflood bulb develops quite a bit of heat, it should never be placed any closer than 10" from the positive. To determine the duration of exposure, make a test screen with the positive to be used. The screen is exposed with the positive mounted, in a series of steps. To begin, the image area is shielded with

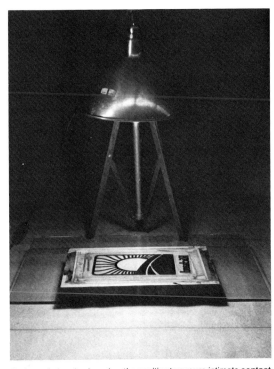

A piece of glass is placed on the positive to ensure intimate contact. When this is achieved, the emulsion is ready for exposure to a light source.

cardboard or similar opaque material so that only $1/6$ of the positive remains uncovered, and is exposed for two minutes to the light source. After the exposure is completed, the cardboard is moved so that another $1/6$ of the image is uncovered. The screen is now exposed to the light source for an additional two minutes. After these two exposures, one area of the screen will have received four minutes of exposure and one area will have received two minutes of exposure. This step-wedge procedure is repeated until the entire image has been exposed in six strips of 2, 4, 6, 8, 10 and 12 minute exposures. The proper exposure time is easily selected by simply looking at the test screen and determining which strip appears most accurate.

Adhesive mounting photographic positive. The fabric side of the emulsion coated screen is sprayed with a thin coat of contact cement—any of the several types available for mounting photographs will work. The spray coating is dried for three to four minutes.

The positive, reading backwards, is gently rubbed down, removing any air bubbles.

Light source for exposure. The light source for the exposure can be a standard 150W reflector flood bulb. This bulb can be mounted in any fixture that allows for positioning and controlling distance between the bulb and the coated screen with the positive.

A general rule for determining light placement is to measure the diagonal of the image and place the light at this distance.

A step-wedge light test. The exposures made will have areas with 2, 4, 6, 8, 10, and 12 minute exposures.

To begin, the image area is shielded with cardboard so that only $1/6$ of the positive remains uncovered and is exposed for 2 minutes to the light source.

After the first 2-minute exposure is complete, the cardboard is moved so that an additional $1/6$ of the image is uncovered. This procedure is repeated until the entire image has been exposed in six strips of exposures.

The proper exposure time is selected by determining which of the six steps appears most accurate.

CHAPTER 4

The photographic stencil is capable of realizing image needs not possible with other screen techniques. To be precise, *any* opaque mark or shape placed on a transparent or translucent film can be made into a photo stencil. A stencil is termed photographic because the materials used to make the stencil are light sensitive.

We have described the hand preparation of photo stencils. At this point, we will explore a few of the numerous possibilities offered by repro-photography.

Too many artists are bewildered by these processes and dismiss them as unaesthetic and impersonal. While this is certainly a valid prerogative, it implies that the personal touch is lost because the methods are mechanical and complex. There is no reason why the artist cannot understand and thereby gain control of these tools in the same way he controls a brush, a burin, a squeegee or a camera. Personal involvement is lost only when the artist loses control of his medium by not understanding it. A knowledge of these methods can broaden and enrich aesthetic expression immeasurably. Twentieth Century science and technology have given us new and improved tools to extend the limits of control. We have been presented with the means for achieving effects not possible otherwise.

HALFTONE

In this chapter, we will present an overview as an introduction to some photo-mechanical processes. In Chapter VI, we will illustrate the implementation of these techniques.

The halftone process evolved to fill the need for a system of printing which could preserve the appearance of all the grays in a black and white photograph. Stencils, of course, share with other printing methods the principle of "print or not print" one density at a time.

The ordinary black and white photograph you take with your camera does not have a half-tone dot. The transition from very dark blacks and grays to very light grays and white is made with no obvious break in continuity. Because it uses a silver base material, it functions as a continuous tone medium. Unfortunately, these continuous tones cannot be duplicated by any single printing process, since all printing techniques are capable of depositing only one density of ink.

The quality defined as black is based upon an object reflecting very little or none of the light falling on it. Conversely, a white object is reflecting most of the light falling upon it. Black and white represent two ends of a spectrum. However, most objects we see are neither black nor white, they fall within the infinite number of grays that bridge the visual space between these two extremes. The halftone process is based upon meeting the need for grays through the principle whereby a pattern small enough to be at the eye's separation threshold will create diffusion on the retina which may convince the eye it is seeing something that is not actually there. Translated practically, if on a specific area of white, a pattern of black dots is placed, and the black dots are small enough, the eye will see neither black nor white, but will discern the area as a value of gray, determined by the proportion of black dots relative to the white area.

The illustration has been printed on white paper with black ink. Although it is not visually perfect, it can readily be accepted as nine values of gray.

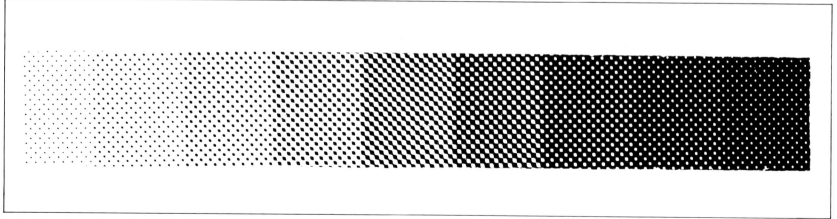

The illustration above has been printed on white paper with black ink. It can easily be accepted as nine values of gray. We can create values between black and white by placing a black dot within a white area so that the eye will generate the percentage of gray optically.

65 line screen

100 line screen

Dot Structure: We know that we can create values between black and white by placing a black dot within a white area so that the eye will generate the percentage of gray optically.

Percentage of Dot: Starting with a one inch white square, we can calculate 30% of the total area and place a black dot representing that amount of the area in the center of the square. Since we can say that 30% of the total area is black and that 70% of the area is white, we would, therefore, have a 30% dot represented. Proceeding to the other end of the scale, using the one inch square, we calculate 70% of the area and make a black dot of that size. This gives us a 70% dot, or black area and a 30% white area. The notion of dot percentage terms the first instance a 30% dot and the second a 70% dot, i.e., percentage of black.

Line Count: The second element in halftones is line count. Line count really means number of lines of dots per inch. The eye being a very refined instrument, will not be convinced that by occupying 30% of a one inch square with a black dot it is seeing gray. To be optically convincing we draw 100 parallel black lines running in both directions on the one inch square—the same area relationship we discussed in the earlier example of the dot. However, this approaches the eye's threshold to separate and therefore represents a gray value more convincingly. Since line tends to have a visual directional pull, we overcome this by continuing one step further. The grid pattern on the one inch square breaks the square into 10,000 small squares (100 x 100). By placing a dot in each of the 10,000 squares (each representing 30% of its small square area) and removing the grid we would have 10,000 dots— representing 30% of the area of the one inch square. This could be considered a 30% gray value. We have illustrated the fundamental concept of line count, and a 30% dot. Since we were using 100 lines of dots per inch, we have an example of a 100 line dot, representing a 30% value. Thus, line count refers to the number of lines of dots per linear inch.

Halftone printing depends upon photographic processes that can assign an appropriate size dot, relative to the white area around it, to represent any gray values found in a normal black and white photograph. As a matter of fact, most photographs in magazines and newspapers, both black and white and color, depend upon this principle.

We recommend that the reader concern himself with printing a halftone only after becoming thoroughly familiar with all the basic hand methods, as well as the photographic stencil. Since most artists have neither the equipment nor the materials to make a halftone positive, we suggest you consult the Yellow Pages under the heading "Photo Copy" for a company that specializes in reproductive photography for the printing trades.

Although the process of making a halftone from a continuous tone photograph is much too complex to completely cover, we will examine the principle without becoming unduly technical. We will begin by asking that you look at an ordinary black and white photograph (choose one either you or a friend has taken), preferably with a magnifying glass. If it is a fairly good photograph, you will see a wide range of grays, with no apparent break in gradation, and certainly no halftone dots. Next, look at a picture in your local newspaper (again, a magnifying glass helps). The halftone dot should be very apparent. The newspaper picture conveys the impression of grays and black and white, but it is actually only black ink on white paper. Your eye has done the job of mixing to imply grays; this is known as visual color mixing. In this instance, black and white are optically combined to form gray. Pictures in magazines, newspapers and other printed material begin as continuous tone, or dotless photographs; the dot is created by a special photographic process. A repro-camera is the basic tool for halftone and other photographic processes intended for reproduction.

Repro-cameras are engineered to perform the operations required to convert an image into a form which is suitable for later printing operations. The repro-camera is composed of three elements: the

copy board, the lens board, and the film holder.
1) The copy board holds the piece to be photographed. It generally has a lighting system as an integral part, designed to evenly light the surface.
2) The lens board holds the lens. Both the lens board and the copy board are movable in relation to each other. This allows an original image to be made larger (blown up) or smaller (reduced).
3) The film holder describes itself. It holds the film in a fixed position and receives the image of the object held on the copy board as transmitted by the lens.

In order to make a halftone, the continuous tone photograph is placed in the copy board and the copy board and lens board are adjusted to achieve the proper image size. Kodalith (or similar high contrast type) film is then placed in the film holder and a halftone contact screen is placed over this. An exposure is made by bouncing light off the original continuous tone photograph in the copy board, through the lens, through the halftone contact screen which is registered on the film. This principle is exactly the same principle employed by a 35 mm hand-held camera. Light is bounced off objects, passed through the lens of the camera and is registered on film held in the camera. There is the one additional element, a halftone contact screen. What is it and why does it work? Upon close inspection, the halftone contact screen resembles a grid pattern where each dot has varying degrees of transparency, graduating into transparent centers.

Density becomes an important consideration at this point. An ordinary black and white continuous tone negative is actually a mask having varying densities. If you hold the negative up to a light source, you notice that the areas that are black in the photograph are transparent in the negative. They allow almost all the light to pass through. These areas have very little "density". The areas in the negative, that represent whites or light grays allow very little light to be transmitted. Therefore, they are considered to have high density. This reversal of values explains why a negative is called a negative. Most photo-

graphic films or papers darken or become black in proportion to the amount of light striking the film in any given area. This means that when you are taking a photograph with your camera, objects reflecting most of the light falling on them (those that are near-white or white), will darken the film, or add density to the film to a greater extent than will darker objects. Objects that are black or in deep shadow, reflect almost no light and the film, therefore, remains virtually clear or without density. Most black and white photography is a two-step process. The first, the negative, is made with a camera and the second, the print, is made on photographic paper using the negative as a mask.

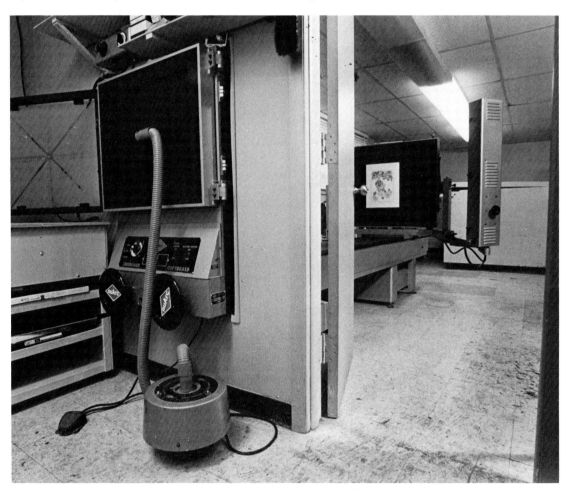

The process camera. The repro-camera is engineered to perform the operations required to convert an image into a form which is suitable for later printing operations. The repro-camera is composed of—the copy board, the lens board, and the film holder. This repro-camera is at the New York Institute of Technology Fine Arts Center in Old Westbury, Long Island, New York.

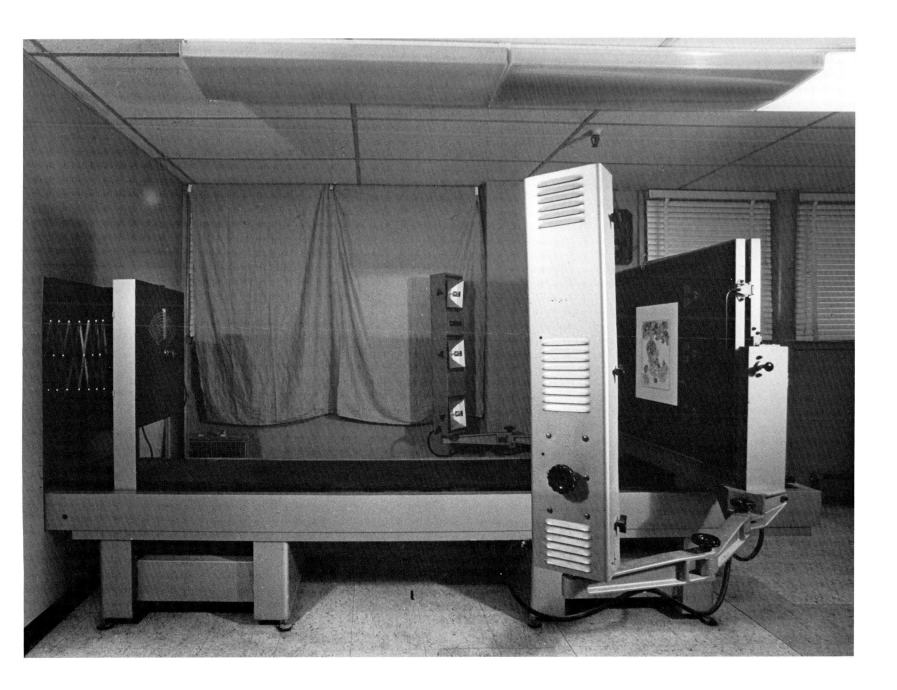

Let's imagine a situation where a photo-sensitive paper is placed under a negative and the two are held sandwich-like in close contact. This sandwich is exposed to a light source so that light must pass through the negative before striking the photo-sensitive paper. As defined, the negative has acquired density or opaqueness in the areas representing the white or light areas of the object photographed. This density or opaqueness in the negative will prevent light from penetrating onto the surface of the photographic paper below. The paper, will, therefore, remain light or white, corresponding to the whiteness or lightness of the object originally photographed. Conversely, it should be obvious that the areas in the negative representing dark areas or areas of shadow have little or no density and will allow most of the light to penetrate the negative and reach the photographic paper below, forming blacks or dark grays on the photographic paper. Our explanation is intended to be as simple and basic as possible. It really says very little about the total photographic process or the many varied possibilities of this exquisite graphic process.

The halftone contact screen works on this very same principle of light penetrating or not penetrating (the varying dot densities). Let's look at an enlargement of an average halftone contact screen.

As the close-up indicates, the halftone contact screen is composed of a clear film base with a pigmented or dye surface which has varying thicknesses, or densities like a funnel. As you can see, the center of any given dot is very thin, or has little density, and permits low levels of light to pass. Density increases progressively as you move out from the center of the dot. This means, in effect, that light must be progressively stronger if it is to penetrate the increasing density it meets as you move out from the center of the dot. As we discovered in the illustration of the negative and photo paper, a weak light source can only penetrate low density. Therefore, we conclude that a weak light source will only form a small dot on the surface of the film below the contact screen. To prove this point, let's return to the object

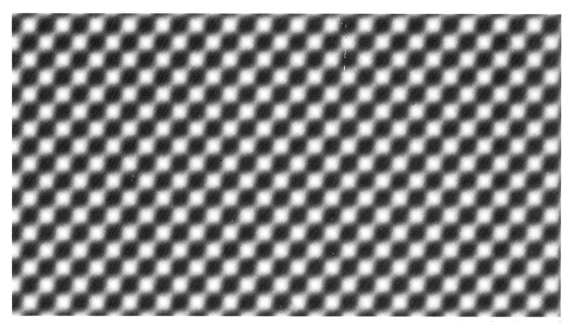

A halftone contact screen. The halftone contact screen is composed of a clear film base with a pigmented surface with varying densities, like a funnel. The center of each dot has little density—it permits low levels of light to pass. Density increases as you move out from the center of the dot. Light must be progressively stronger being photographed in the repro-camera and imagine to penetrate the increasing density moving out from the center of the dot. A weak light source can only penetrate the low density center. Therefore, a weak light source will only form a small dot on the surface of the film below the contact screen.

being photographed in the repro-camera and imagine a relatively dark gray area on it, we know such an area on the original will reflect very little of the light falling on it. Since the light this dark gray area can transmit through the lens will be weak, we surmise that it will only penetrate the center, or low density area, of the contact screen. Thus, it will form a very small dot on the film under the contact screen. On the other hand, areas that are white or light gray values will reflect most of the light falling on them. These areas will transmit a far stronger light source through the lens and will be capable of penetrating the thicker densities on the contact screen and, therefore, will form a larger dot on the photographic film held under the contact screen. But wait, something is wrong! After the film is developed, we find that the areas reflecting little light (those that were dark gray or black in the original from which the half-tone was made) now have a small dot and appear light, while the areas that were light on the original have a large dot and appear dark. We have a reversal of the original object photographed or simply put, a negative. This negative, placed in contact with an unexposed piece of photographic paper or film and exposed to a light source, will reverse so that the relationship of light and dark will correspond to the values in the original. More significant, the blacks in a halftone positive are all black and any illusion of gray is created by the relationship of the area of the black dot to the area of the clear film around it. For the sake of clarity, our discussion has not dealt with the wide variety of contact screens available or, more importantly, the great control that can be exercised by a sensitive and competent camera man.

Continuous tone photo.

The same photograph, after exposure with a halftone screen.

PHOTO POSTERIZATION

In our investigation of the halftone principle, we discussed the idea of converting a continuous tone image into an image having one density but varying in area relationships of density and non-density in order to simulate a continuous tone. Photo-posterization utilizes the unique properties of certain high-contrast films made specifically for photo-reproduction. Such photo-mechanical film is made specifically to eliminate all values of gray. They see, literally, in black and white (Kodak Kodalith, GAF P-407, Agfa Gevalith). A continuous tone negative is placed in the copy board of the repro-camera. The high contrast Kodalith film used will respond very precisely to levels of reflected light, since this film has the characteristic of being virtually blind to gradations of tonal qualities. The image resulting on the film is a product of (1) the length of exposure to light and (2) the type and length of development. Assuming the type and length of development are constant, we will make four negatives from the continuous tone negative in the copy board. The first exposure (period of time the piece receives light with the lens open) will be short. Because the film is exceptionally critical in its recording, the first exposure will record only those areas that reflect a high level of the light falling on it. When another exposure is made with the duration of exposure time increased, it will record the very light areas recorded in the first exposure plus areas that are darker in value. This occurs because the film responds to the amount of light it receives. This process can be continued in as many steps as necessary. By progressively increasing exposure time, the film progressively records the reflected light working from lighter to darker.

These exposures form a series of negatives recording reflected light values corresponding to the number of negatives exposed. If these negatives are contacted back on film to make positives, of a value of gray corresponding to the gray the film positive represents, the original can be reconstructed. Stencils are made from each of the positives and the correct gray can then be printed through these sten-

The silver based negative of this continuous tone photograph was used to produce the four posterized positives on page 35.

After placing the negative into an enlarger, the image has been exposed onto Kodalith film. By using four different exposure times, four different value levels are recorded on the film. These four exposures represent four distinct values seen as different densities in the negative. After posterized positives have been produced, photographic screens can be made. The positives represent different percentages of the total image.

cils. This will create an image similar to the original, but with edges between the grays. The image formed cannot be called continuous tone, because the grays do not flow into one another, but terminate in edges. From the creative viewpoint, the reader should be aware that a black and white photograph can be separated in this manner and reassembled in the printing process by using color in place of gray. If the values (light and dark) of the colors selected conform to the values of the area that the stencil represents, the printed image will work in terms of light and dark despite the fact that the colors have been changed. This process offers many possibilities for experimentation and can be a direct route to dramatic graphic effects with color without dots appearing in the final print.

In another section, we will demonstrate how a print can be made using this method. The posterized separations are relatively simple to make. Nonetheless, we suggest that you supply a repro-photographer with the piece to be photographed and have him make the photographic positives.

FOUR-COLOR PROCESS

We have briefly explained the halftone system as a printing compromise to achieve a full scale of grays between black and white. This system is not a color method but a method for producing value (light and dark). Can we produce a seemingly full range of colors without printing hundreds of colors? An ingenious answer prompted by necessity is the four-color process. As we have discovered, if halftone dots are small enough to be undetectable at an average viewing distance, the eye mixes the black of the dot and the white of the paper to form a gray. Let's consider a situation where in a given area, we use not one but two dots. Let's make one of the dots red and the other yellow. The eye will visually mix the red dot and the yellow dot and the white of the paper to form an orange which falls between the red and the yellow. The size of the red dot and the yellow dot in relation to each other will determine the redness or the yellowness of the orange. If the red dot is large in

relation to the area, and the yellow dot small, the orange visualized will be a very red orange. If the reverse is true, the red dot being small and the yellow dot large, the orange visualized will be a very yellow orange. Keep in mind that these dots are usually printed on a white surface which is another factor to consider. The redness or yellowness of the orange are determined by the relation of the dot sizes to each other. But, the saturation or strength of the orange depends upon the total area of the red and the yellow dot in relation to the amount of white surrounding them. Put differently, within a given area of white (dependent upon the line count of half-tone screen used), if the red dot and yellow dot are large and the white area remaining is small, the orange created will be very bright or saturated. If in that same area of white, the red dot and yellow dot occupy very little area, the resulting orange will appear as a very weak or pastel orange. This is a simple illustration of the principle of visual color mixing. We have only talked about two colors thus far. However, in order to print a visually acceptable full range of colors, four colors are generally used.

1) Red—the red used is called magenta, which is a cool red with a bluish cast
2) Yellow—the yellow used is called yellow in the process and is a somewhat greenish yellow
3) Blue—the blue used is called cyan, and has a greenish cast
4) Black—is called black in the process and is a cool black

We definitely do not recommend that the beginning or even the intermediate screen printer become involved in the four-color process. Nevertheless, we do wish to explain how the necessary positives, or color separations are made. The object to be photographed is placed in a repro-camera; but whereas the halftone in the previous example was photographed from a black and white object, the object photographed now is in full color.

First, the original is taken apart and made into four negatives that represent the four colors that will be printed later—magenta, yellow, cyan and black. The

singling out of a particular color is accomplished by the use of color filters. The film used for this purpose forms what appears to be a black and white negative. Actually, there will be no color in the negative, but instead a representation by density of the saturation of the particular color being photographed. The film being used to make the negative must be sensitive to the same range of the color spectrum that the eye perceives.

Color Filters: If a red piece of glass is held up to a white light source, the light passing through the red glass to the eye is red. White light is composed primarily of red, blue and green. What happens to the red glass? Why is it red? We have white light striking one side of the glass. However, since the light is composed of red, blue and green, the red glass, due to its pigmentation or absorption quality, will not transmit the blue light or the green light. The only color which passes is the red, therefore, to the eye, the glass is red.

Color filters are light barriers that permit selected light frequencies to pass. Therefore, since the film involved sees much the same as the eye, by selecting the proper color filter we can controlably select that area of the color spectrum we want the film to see. In this manner, negatives are made representing the proper densities for magenta, yellow, cyan and black. These negatives are used to make the positives. When making the positive, a halftone contact screen is used which produces a positive with a halftone dot. The halftone dot will represent an area of color in relation to surrounding white that conforms to the value of color in the original. When these four halftone positives, each representing one of the four necessary colors, are reassembled in the printing process, the resulting image will be a visually acceptable representation of natural color. Unlike posterization, the dots are a part of the finished print.

Moire Patterns: This is a phenomenon that occurs when two patterns are placed, one upon the other, so that a third pattern is created. This third pattern is called a moire pattern, and is caused by the

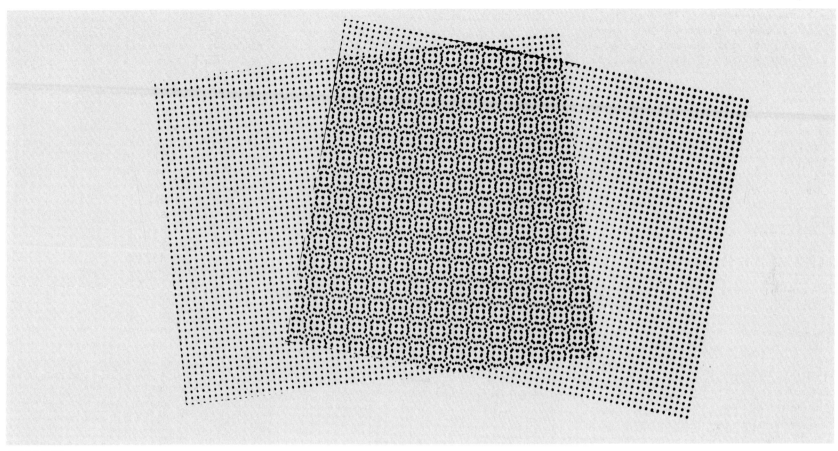

Moire pattern.

interference of one pattern with the other in a somewhat symmetrical order.

This effect is interesting, optically, but when unintentional it can play havoc with an image. We mention this because we have just discussed four-color printing which employs four or more patterns or dots. Should a moire pattern occur, entirely unwanted effects may be created (wavy lines, etc.). To control this, the repro-photographer angles the lines of dots at very specific intervals to each other to eliminate moire patterns. We suggest that you examine this

point for yourself by acquiring a sheet of Benday dot pattern from an art supply store. Cut this sheet in half, and by moving one half over the other, moire patterns will be created and the moire principle will be visually demonstrated.

The moire principle is also important when printing a one color halftone. The halftone positive is a regularly patterned system of dots. This alone does not offer a problem. However, when this positive is used to make a stencil in a screen which has its own regular pattern of threads and openings, the two

regular patterns, halftone positive and screen fabric, can generate a moire. This requires the angle of dot in the halftone to be carefully oriented to the angle of the thread to minimize moire. This is accomplished by placing the halftone positive on a lighted surface, placing the screen on top of the positive and rotating the screen in relation to the positive until the moire is at a minimum. The screen is marked (using Magic Marker, etc.) so the positive can be placed in the same position for exposure after the screen has been coated with photo-emulsion and dried.

CHAPTER 5

Producing a screen print can be thought of as a two stage process. A screen mounted with a stencil is prepared, after which the printing operation is performed. Of the total time spent in making a screen print most is devoted (like this book) to screen and stencil preparation. Almost anyone can learn to pull a squeegee, since no unusual skill is involved. As you will see, it is a simple mechanical operation.

REGISTRATION & PRINTING

Before the printing operation is begun, you must have a screen, with a stencil mounted by hinges to a printing base. We know that the screen, when lowered for printing will always come down in the same position relative to the base. We must now employ a system for placing consecutive sheets of paper beneath the screen, so that each can assume the same relative position to the image on the stencil, in registration.

Three-Point Registration: The most convenient and commonly used registration method is known as the three-point registration system. Paper is placed on the printing base in the desired position relative to the image in the screen. Two pieces of masking tape hold the sheet of paper in place, while the registration points are mounted. These registration tabs can be made from thin, stiff cardboard or thin plastic. The registration tabs are taped to the printing base with masking tape as shown in the illustration.

One edge of each of the registration tabs is in light contact with an edge of the properly placed sheet of paper. If the masking tape that temporarily held the paper is removed, the sheet of paper can also be removed with the guarantee that any sheet of paper subsequently placed under the screen against these registration tabs will have its two edges registered in the same relative position to the image in the stencil.

Precise registration is crucial when printing two or more colors. Each color is printed through a separate stencil or, in other words, one color is printed completely and then the next color is printed. Registration becomes critical in printing the second color (and subsequent colors) which must fall into a specific area relative to the earlier color(s) printed. However, if the three-point registration system is used carefully, with the same points on the edge of the sheet, there should be little difficulty with registration.

One edge of each registration tab is in contact with an edge of the paper. The masking tape that temporarily held the paper is removed. This sheet can be removed with the assurance that any sheet of paper placed under the screen against these tabs will be registered in the same relative position to the image in the stencil.

Three-point registration. Paper is placed on the printing base in position. Masking tape holds the sheet of paper in place, while registration points are mounted. Registration tabs can be made from thin, stiff cardboard or thin plastic. The tabs are taped to the base with masking tape, as shown.

Transparent flap overlay registration. For materials which do not lend themselves to the three-point registration system. A transparent plastic or mylar can be used. The first color must be printed on the material. After this, the stencil for the second color is set up.

Transparent-Flap-Overlay Registration:

Some materials, like fabrics, do not lend themselves to the three-point registration system. In these instances, the flap overlay method of registration can be called into use. Flap registration employs a transparent or transluscent material such as clear plastic or tracing paper to register second and subsequent colors. This registration system requires that the first color be printed on the material. After this, the stencil for the second color is set up on the printing base. A sheet of plastic or tracing paper is taped to the printing base along one edge. This flap material must be large enough in relation to the taped edge to assure that the taped edge will not interfere with the placement of the material to be printed. When the flap material is in position, the stencil image is printed directly on it. We suggest that the printed image be dried by raising the screen (when dry, it may be necessary to wash the image area of the stencil with the proper solvent and then dry it with paper towels). The dry, printed flap is carefully lifted so it is not loosened from the printing base. The material to be printed is then placed under the flap so that the image first printed on the material and the image subsequently printed on the flap are in alignment or "registration" with each other. The flap is carefully folded back so it does not interfere with contact between the stencil and the material being printed. Again, care must be exercised so that the flap is not loosened from the printing base. The printing may then proceed. Because the image on the flap is in register with the image in the stencil, it is possible to use the flap to position the material being printed so that the material is also registered to the image on the stencil.

A sheet of mylar is taped along one edge. This flap material must be large enough to assure that the taped edge will not interfere with placing the material to be printed. The stencil image is printed directly on the flap.

The material being printed is placed under the flap so that the image on the material and on the flap are in register. The flap is folded back so that it will not interfere with contact between the stencil and the material being printed.

PRINTING

Before the printing is begun it is important that all required material be conveniently at hand. This includes the squeegee, the ink, a roll of masking tape, scissors, newspaper, a roll of paper towels and the correct solvent for the ink. After the stencil has been made and the screen properly set up on the printing base, the printing operation is quite simple.

Off-Contact Method: Most screen printers employ the "off-contact" technique of printing. This involves creating a situation whereby the screen, when lowered to the printing position does not make contact with the paper or other material below it until it is forced down by the squeegee. The off-contact printing situation is created by inserting pieces of cardboard under the hinge bar in the rear and taping small strips of cardboard to the two front bottom corners of the screen frame itself. This keeps the screen, when lowered to the printing position from touching the surface below by being slightly off-contact, by about 1/8″. Because the screen does not touch the paper until forced down by the squeegee, the printed edges will be cleaner and sharper with off-contact printing. When a screen is not off-contact, it means that ink left in the screen from printing the first sheet of paper will very likely be transferred to the second sheet, so that when the squeegee is pulled across a double image can result.

Flood Stroke and Printing Stroke: To begin the actual printing operation, an adequate amount of the ink being used is poured into the screen along the right hand side. The screen is raised 1–2 inches and the squeegee used to pull the ink from the right hand side to the left hand side of the screen (or top to bottom on top-hinged screens) leaving a thin film of ink on top of the stencil. This is called the "flood stroke"—its purpose is to fill the open stencil image with ink. The screen may then be raised and allowed to rest on the kick-leg. A sheet of paper is positioned under the screen in contact with the registration tabs. The screen is lowered gently to the printing position. The squeegee is used to pull the ink back across the

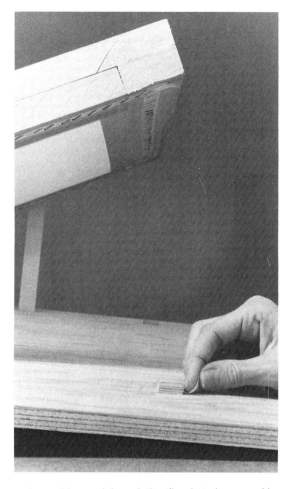

Off contact. Insert pieces of cardboard under the hinge bar in rear and tape small strips of cardboard in line with the two front corners of the screen frame. The screen, when lowered, will not touch the surface below because it is slightly off contact—approximately 1/8″.

screen with a firm, steady stroke. This forces the ink through the stencil and prints the image on the paper, or other material under the stencil; this is called the "printing stroke". Next, the screen is raised an inch or two from the front and the squeegee is again used to pull the ink from the right to the left hand side of the screen in a flood stroke. The screen is raised and allowed to rest on the kick-leg. The printed sheet is removed and set aside to dry. A second sheet is placed on the printing board resting against the regis-

tration guides and the printing flood stroke sequel is repeated. This is continued until the desired number of images have been printed.

When pulling the squeegee across the screen, in either the printing or flood stroke, the squeegee should be angled about 15 to 20 degrees off the vertical in the direction of the stroke. This allows the printing to be done by one edge of the squeegee blade. This will result in a much cleaner impression than if the flat surface of the blade is used.

The printing operation begins with ink poured into the screen. The screen is raised 1 to 2 inches and the squeegee pulls the ink from one side to the other side of the screen leaving a thin film of ink on top of the stencil. This is the flood stroke. Its purpose is to fill the open stencil image with ink. The screen is allowed to rest on the kick-leg. A sheet of paper is positioned under the screen in contact with the registration tabs.

Printing stroke. The squeegee is used to pull the ink back across the screen with a firm, steady stroke which forces the ink through the stencil and prints the image on the paper. After which the screen is again raised an inch or two and the squeegee used to pull across the screen in a flood stroke.

When pulling the squeegee across the screen in either printing or flood stroke, the squeegee should be angled about 15-20° off the vertical in the direction of the stroke so that the printing is done by one edge of the squeegee blade.

Reclaiming Screens: After the printing operations, screens should be thoroughly cleaned and stencils removed. This will leave an open screen in which future stencils can be placed.

Immediately after finishing the printing, all ink should be removed from the screen, placed back in the ink container and sealed. If solvent ink was used, the screen is placed on a pad of newspaper and the solvent for the ink poured into the screen. Paper towels are used to spread the solvent and pick up the remaining ink. This should be repeated three to four times to insure that all ink has been removed. The newspaper, under the screen, should be changed frequently because it absorbs ink passing through the stencil. When all ink has been removed from the screen, solvent soaked newspaper and paper towels should be disposed of in a covered metal container such as a garbage can.

Next we must remove the stencil so that the mesh of the screen is entirely opened.

Methods of Stencil Removal:

1) The paper stencil will come off in the wash up operation and no special removal procedures are needed unless glue has been used to attach areas. If glue has been used, remove the glue areas with the proper solvent.

2) The direct block-out stencil is washed with the appropriate solvent for the block-out material—hot water procedure for water soluble block-out, lacquer for lacquer soluble block-out. Hot water procedure—soak in hot water and Spic and Span for 10 minutes. Use approximately two tablespoons of detergent per quart of hot water.

3) Tusche & glue block-out material is water soluble and again very hot water is used to remove it. A hand spray makes this a simple operation.

4) Most photographic stencils use the same removal procedure. All ink is first removed from the photographic stencil. A hot water spray will remove any block-out material that may have been used over the photo stencil. This also will swell the photographic emulsion and make it more receptive to a chlorine bleach, such as Clorox, which is then applied. It is important to use "fresh" bleach. We caution you to wear rubber gloves during this procedure and to avoid splashing the bleach on yourself or your clothing. If you do get any bleach on you, wash very thoroughly with cold water. The chlorine bleach is best applied with a stiff nylon brush. After thoroughly brush scrubbing both sides of the stencil, allow the screen to stand for a few minutes. Next, if a flow of hot water from a hand sprayer is directed on to the screen it should remove all stencil residue. The screen is then dried and when dry, held up to a light source or window for examination to insure that all ink and stencil material has been removed. Should residue remain, it can be removed by scrubbing the screen with a strong solvent such as acetone. (Acetone is sold at paint and hardware stores.) Extreme caution should be exercised with the use of acetone. Follow manufacturers instructions with extreme care to avoid problems.

CHAPTER 6

A screen print is the result of a sequence of operations: stencil preparation, color formulation, and printing. These procedures are interdependent, because alone, none is capable of providing all the elements required for the printed image form. The stencil, of course, determines the areas which are printed. However, by ink and color selection, some modifications of an image can be achieved during printing. In this chapter we will deal with the interrelationship of these operations.

By producing screen prints using each of the stencil types we hope to amplify the reader's understanding of the stencil as the critical intermediate stage between concept and final print. Thus, screen printing will be revealed as both a flexible means for transposing an idea into an image, and as a medium whose characteristics can significantly contribute to the visual form of an idea.

HAND-CUT PAPER STENCILS

As we have mentioned, a hand-cut paper stencil can be made of any strong, thin paper like tracing paper, drawing paper, or layout bond.

There are advantages in using hand-cut paper stencils rather than hand-cut film stencils. Paper is inexpensive and readily available. In addition, a paper stencil can be quickly and simply attached to a screen. These assets must be weighed against the paper stencil's disadvantages. Paper stencils make maintaining accurate registration of more than one color difficult because of stencil shifting. Paper stencils must be rather simple because their lack of durability tends to cause them to fray during printing. Using a thick paper does not alleviate this problem, since edges of a thick paper stencil will fray because of the bleeding of ink during the printing operation. Also, a paper stencil can become saturated with ink during printing, which makes the stencil slacken or wrinkle. This means it is often impossible to salvage it for use in printing other colors.

We should consider certain effects the paper stencil can achieve which the hand-cut film stencil cannot. These include—tearing the paper to create interesting edge properties; using porous paper so that ink can bleed through the stencil for interesting textural effects.

HAND-CUT FILM STENCIL

Basically, a hand-cut film stencil when printed will have the same quality as a paper stencil. However, there are distinct advantages in using stencil film to prepare a hand-cut stencil . . . Three advantages are:

1) stencil film is durable, it can sustain a large number of impressions

2) any interior areas (islands), remain in position during the adhering operation, because they are attached to a plastic carrier sheet

3) very fine detail can be maintained.

We will print the "O" stencil we discussed in Chapter III. But first, let's review the procedure for making a hand-cut film stencil. You begin by cutting a piece of stencil film slightly larger than the image to be printed. This piece of film is positioned over the art work and taped down. Because the film is transparent, the drawing will be visible. Since hand-cut film is composed of a thin layer of film bonded to a carrier sheet or clear plastic backing you must always place it on the drawing so that the film side is facing up—not the plastic backing sheet. The film side can be determined by cutting a small square in a corner of the film and then peeling the film away from the backing. Doing this will avoid the distress you can feel after spending time and energy cutting a stencil, only to discover that you have cut the plastic backing and not the film! It is essential to use an extremely sharp knife for cutting. But, be careful not to cut the film so deeply that you cut into the plastic carrier. After the film is correctly positioned over the drawing, the film is cut, and the areas to be printed are peeled away. The hand-cut film stencil can then be placed beneath the clean screen to which it will be attached. Positive contact between the hand-cut film and the clean screen is absolutely necessary. To achieve this, you should cut several pieces of cardboard larger than the hand-cut film, but smaller than the inside dimension of the screen. This cardboard is placed under the hand-cut film. When the screen is positioned and weighted atop the hand-cut film, the cardboard will insure intimate contact between the hand-cut film and clean screen. The stencil can then be attached to the screen fabric with the appropriate solvent. The manufacturer's instructions for the particular stencil film should be carefully read and followed. After adhering, the screen/film combination should remain in a weighted position until dry. A fan will assist in removing solvents. After the screen is dry, the open area on the screen fabric between the edges of the stencil film and the wooden frame should be closed with a screen filler or block-out material. Remember to use a filler material which is soluble in the same solvent as the hand-cut film. With one solvent removing both the film and the blockout, reclaiming the screen for further use is made easier.

After the first coat of screen filler is thoroughly dry (again, a fan helps), the plastic backing sheet can be lifted at a corner and peeled away from the cut film. We then suggest a second coat of screen filler be applied. This second coat of filler should overlap the outside edge of the stencil film slightly. Once more, carefully avoid filling in the open areas of the screen that will be printed.

The printing area is prepared and all necessary supplies are arranged to be easily accessible. The ink is selected and paper is cut to proper size. A sheet of paper of the same dimensions as those to be printed, is placed beneath the stencil and moved about until the image in the screen falls on the area of the paper you want printed. After this is accomplished the paper should be taped into place on the printing base. The guides (we use small, thin, plastic guides) are taped into the three-point registration position. The paper can now be removed.

The hand-cut stencil "0" printed.

The direct block-out stencil printed in opaque magenta ink.

Block-out stencil (opaque magenta) printed over hand-cut film stencil "0" (yellow).

A piece of paper to be printed is placed in position against the guides and a small amount of ink is poured into the top of the screen. The screen is lifted one or two inches and the squeegee is used to draw the ink across the screen in the flood stroke. The screen is lowered to the printing position and the squeegee is used to perform the printing stroke. After printing, the screen is again raised several inches so that the ink can be squeegeed back across the screen in the flood stroke, after which the screen is allowed to rest on the kick leg. At this point, the printed piece can be removed and inspected. If everything regarding image and color appears suitable, the printed image is set aside to dry and a second piece of paper is positioned. The same procedures (flooding, printing, flooding, and removal of printed image) are again performed. This sequence is repeated until the total number of desired images has been printed.

At the end of the printing operation place 8–10 sheets of newspaper under the screen and lower the screen to the printing position. A piece of stiff cardboard should be used to scoop excess ink from the screen which is returned to its container. Then, using the proper solvent for the ink, remove remaining ink from the screen with pads of paper towels. When using other than water soluble inks, this washing operation is repeated with clean paper towels and clean newspapers under the screen 3–4 times to be absolutely certain all ink has been removed from the screen. The screen filler, because it is soluble in the same solvent as the ink, will also be removed during this operation.

To remove the film stencil from the screen—place 3–4 sheets of newspaper under the screen and sprinkle them with lacquer thinner. Lower the screen and sprinkle lacquer thinner on the screen fabric. Make a paper towel pad and use it to rub down the screen to dissolve the stencil. Lift the screen and the newspaper will come with it. When you peel away the newspaper stuck to the screen, much of the dis-solved stencil will come off with it. This clean-up operation should be repeated until the screen is clear of all but a few spots or a haze. Then the screen is placed in a vertical position. Two paper towel pads are saturated with thinner and used to rub both sides of the screen simultaneously. Replace the pads as they become stained and continue rubbing until all traces of the stencil are removed. Stubborn areas will require acetone.

DIRECT BLOCK-OUT STENCIL

The second print will be produced using the block-out stencil. This stencil can allow the artist to take advantage of printing on the first color—the yellow "O."

Referring to the "O" printed through the hand-cut film stencil, the image on the block-out stencil is transferred to one of the sheets upon which we have printed the first color. This is done in the form of a loose drawing made with a dark pencil.

This drawing is placed beneath the screen, and moved about until it is in register with the block-out stencil image. Guide points are then taped to the printing base. Remember, all areas on the screen fabric that will *not* be printed have already been filled in with a block-out or screen filler material. Raise the screen and inspect it to insure that non-printing areas are completely blocked out. Using a light source behind the screen will aid this inspection. Screen filler should be applied with a small brush to close off any open areas or pin-spots that you detect. After drying the screen filler, the screen is ready for printing.

Since the guide points were secured when the drawing was positioned beneath the screen, a color can now be printed. We printed a yellow "O" through the cut film stencil. We will print an opaque magenta through the block-out stencil. Thus, we will see magenta where it falls over the yellow used as the first color. We will also print the block-out stencil as a one color image using the same opaque magenta ink we used to print on the "O." Then by using transparent base mixed with the magenta ink, another print is made possible.

Using only two simple stencils we have printed four different pieces. You can easily see that other combinations of these stencils and colors are possible. Again, we emphasize the importance of having all necessary materials at hand before the printing operation is begun. The printing operation is performed in exactly the same way described earlier. The print is positioned against the guides. The screen is lowered, flooded, and printed. The print is removed and inspected for color as well as registration to the previous color printed. At the same time, the print is checked to see if it shows any color leaking through the stencil. Should color leaks be detected, scoop the ink from the screen, then thoroughly wash the screen with the proper solvent and allow it to dry. After this, the leaks can be touched up with the same block-out material previously used.

The block-out stencil image was also printed with magenta ink to which transparent base was added.

TUSCHE-RESIST STENCIL

This stencil method also requires working directly on the screen fabric. Like the block-out stencil, the tusche-resist stencil depends upon the screen mesh being filled in with a block-out material. However, this stencil has the advantage of being a positive working system; the image put into the screen is the image that is actually printed. Tusche lends itself to a loose, drawing approach. We will print the stencil we prepared in Chapter III.

The screen is inspected to be sure the mesh is open in the desired areas. Occasionally, to remove any residual tusche, it is necessary to dampen two pads of paper towels which are used to simultaneously scrub the screen on both sides. When the screen mesh is open and dry, the stencil is ready for printing.

To prepare this stencil, we have used the Hunt/Speedball Drawing Fluid/Block-out system that is totally water soluble and does not require the use of mineral spirits or other solvents aside from water. We drew on the screen with the drawing fluid. When this was dry, we applied the screen filler just as the glue is applied in the traditional tusche-resist method. The screen was left to dry over night. The drawing fluid was removed with a spray of cold water. When dry, the stencil was printed.

The printing operation is identical to that employed for the hand-cut stencil and the direct block-out stencil. Paper is positioned against the guides, the screen is raised to an inch or two, and flooded with ink; the screen is then lowered to the printing position and the printing stroke performed. The screen is again raised an inch or two and flooded, after which it is raised so it is supported by the kick-leg. The print is removed and inspected. If the color and registration are correct, the print is set aside to dry. The remaining pieces are then printed.

We have decided to print this piece in two colors. To facilitate this on the same screen we have blocked out all the areas not being printed by covering these areas, using paper and masking tape. After printing the black form on all the sheets of paper, we cleaned the screen thoroughly, and then blocked out that area of the screen just printed with paper and masking tape. After removing the paper and masking tape from the circular form we can print a second color. First we print red. We clean the screen and then print green. We clean the screen once more and print blue. This provides a visual reference for selecting the second color to printed. This kind of color comparison is one of the unique aesthetic capabilities of the printmaking process.

Blocking out second color on tusche-resist stencil using paper and masking tape.

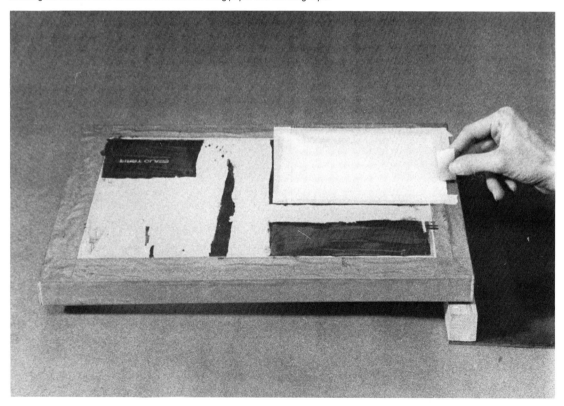

Tusche-resist stencil with first color (black) printed.

FIRST CLASS

46

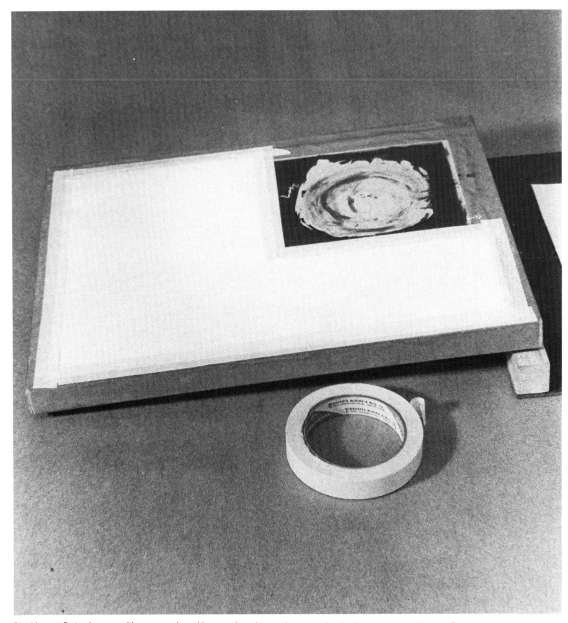

Blocking out first color area with paper and masking tape in order to print second color from tusche-resist stencil.

PHOTOGRAPHIC STENCIL

The photographic stencil is undoubtedly the most versatile of all stencils. As we have mentioned, the stencil is made of light-sensitive material which accounts for the literal derivation of the term "photographic stencil." The photo stencil opens up an almost limitless range of image possibilities. To understand why this is so—consider how a photo stencil is prepared. The screen is coated with an emulsion which is highly sensitive to light. This coating is called a light-hardening emulsion because exposure to light hardens it and makes it insoluble in water. Those parts of the emulsion blocked from light exposure remain soft and can be washed away with water, leaving the screen open for the passage of ink. The mask for blocking light is called the "positive." A positive can be made of any image which can be opaquely placed on a transparent or transluscent sheet. Tracing paper can be used to make a positive, but it sometimes offers problems when a water soluble material such as ink or water color is used as a drawing medium. Acetate or mylar sheets are more stable and lie flatter. Bienfang Paper Co. makes an excellent prepared acetate called Wet Media. It will accept any wet medium—including india ink—

Completed two-color print using tusche-resist method stencil. The circular form was printed as a second color, after the rest of the image had been printed black. After proofing it with red, then green, and then blue as the second color—the choice was made to print the shape in green.

without "crawling." Any material that can be put down opaquely can be used to create the positive on the transparent sheet. For example—inks, paints, photo opaque, pastels, crayons can be applied directly, with brushes, with pens, or by dry brushing, spattering, stippling or sponging to create tonal and textured effects. In addition, commercial dry transfer materials can be used to make photographic positives. These materials are available in an amazingly wide variety of textures, type faces, symbols, borders and designs. There are many different brands, among the most popular are—Zip-atone, Formatt, Lettraset, Prestype, Craftint. These can be found at most art supply stores.

There are two types of commercial dry transfer material available. The rub-down type comes on a sheet which is not removable. The rub-down sheet is placed over the area to be covered and is carefully outlined with a sharp pointed knife. The excess portion of the sheet is removed. The sheet is burnished with a thumbnail or burnishing tool to insure tight adherence to the acetate sheet. The sunrise symbol we have used is a rub-down material manufactered by Formatt.

With the second type of dry transfer, the backing sheet is removed and the transfer sheet positioned to cover the required area. A tool, like a rounded piece of wood or plastic, is used to rub or burnish the transfer sheet. This pressure transfers the image from the plastic sheet. Care must be exercised to burnish only the area where the transfer is desired. The letters for Richard were selected from the many type faces available. The type face is Vintage Bold made by Prestype.

After the acetate sheet is imprinted with an image, the next step is to transfer that image into a screen as a stencil.

The cardinal rule of screen preparation is that the screen used, for this or any other stencil, must be *absolutely clean*. This is so essential, that we will review the procedure. If the screen to be used has been previously involved in any printing operation, all ink must be removed with the proper solvent for that ink. All traces of the stencil which was used must also be removed. The screen fabric, when held up to a lighted window or light source, should be totally open and free of obstructions. Immediately prior to making a new stencil, the screen fabric should be washed with a detergent water solution (dishwasher powder solution) and a nylon bristle brush.

DIRECT PHOTOGRAPHIC STENCIL
Because we so strongly favor the direct photographic stencil for its simplicity and durability, we will review the steps to follow in its preparation.

The material we have used to cover the screen is a bichromate liquid emulsion which comes in a two-part system, the emulsion and the sensitizer. The two components are mixed according to the manufacturer's instructions (again—read the instructions). When mixed, the emulsion is coated on the screen in the following manner: The clean screen is placed on a firm, flat surface with the fabric side up. A small amount of the emulsion is poured across one end of the screen fabric. A squeegee or stiff piece of cardboard is used to spread the emulsion across the fabric with a firm even motion. We suggest that the same squeegee or piece of cardboard be used to coat the screen a second time, moving across in the opposite direction. The screen can then be turned over so that the frame is face up, resting on blocks of wood placed under the screen. A small amount of emulsion is poured along the end of the fabric and spread across the fabric in the same way as the first side.

The screen must be dry before it is exposed to a light source. It should be dried in a horizontal position with the fabric side down (use push pins in frame corners), in a dark room or closet, or an area where the light level is *very* low. A stream of air from a fan, directed across the wet emulsion will accelerate drying. When the emulsion is thoroughly dry (approximately one hour with a fan), you can expose the positive and emulsion to light. Keep in mind that the emulsion is not terribly sensitive to light when wet. However, since its photo-sensitive qualities become pronounced when dry, all of the following operations should be conducted under lighting conditions which will not adversely affect the photo-emulsion. Exposure to direct sunlight or fluorescent light will speedily act on the emulsion and spoil the stencil you are making. This is the result of the fact that the emulsion is primarily sensitive to the ultra-violet rays—the blue end of the light spectrum. Therefore, sunlight which is very rich in blue and most fluorescent bulbs which are moderately rich in blue, can rapidly expose the emulsion. Actually, a 50 or 75 watt tungsten, or ordinary household light bulb placed in a ceiling fixture, should create no problems, allowing the operations to be safely conducted.

Let's review the adhesive method for achieving intimate contact between the positive and the dry emulsion.

Adhesive Mount Method: This mounting method is quite simple. Before you begin, arrange several sheets of newspaper to protect surrounding objects. The screen, fabric side up, is placed in the center of the newspaper and sprayed with a thin coat of photo-type contact adhesive. Spray until you achieve an even mist coating—the objective being a dry but slightly tacky surface. Allow the adhesive to dry two to three minutes. Then you will be ready to mount the prepared positive directly to the photo-emulsion. It is *very* important to remember to mount the positive to the *under*-side of the screen. Since you will be printing the screen from the frame side, the positive must "read" correctly from the frame side of the screen. This simply requires that you place the positive on the fabric side reading backwards. This is guaranteed to work out correctly if you simply remember to place the side of the plastic that you have drawn upon so it is directly against the photo-emulsion.

Light Exposure: The light source for the exposure can be a standard 150 watt reflector flood bulb. This bulb can be mounted in any fixture that allows for positioning and controlling distance between the bulb and the coated screen with the positive

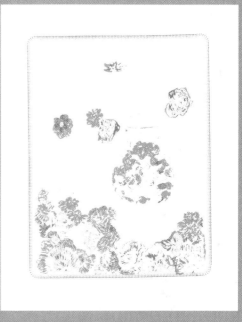

The first color, yellow, printed. This color and all other colors were printed through photo-stencils.

For the second color, transparent base was mixed with light blue ink. Where it falls over the white of the paper, you see light blue. Where it falls on the yellow, a third color—green is created.

The third color printed, a transparent pink. Pink appears where it falls on the white of the paper; orange where it falls on the yellow; violet where it falls on the blue. Thus, by printing only three colors, six colors have been produced.

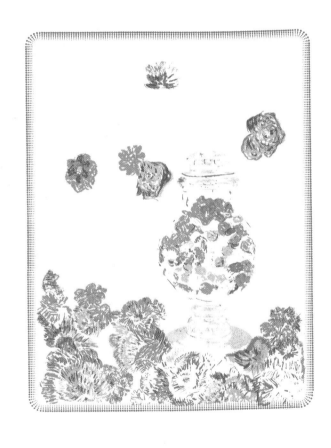

The original collage was used to prepare four posterized steps. Each was printed in a different color. The posterizations have been used to add definition to the three-color printed image.

A half-tone of the original collage was produced. By printing this half-tone over all the colors printed thus far, the image has achieved articulation in terms of value and form.

The finished print. Referring to all the previous colors printed, a line drawing was created. This hand drawn image was transferred photographically into a stencil. This final photo-stencil was printed using green enamel ink.

mounted. Most hardware stores carry a simple clamp-on type bulb holder which works very well. Arrange a set-up using this type of clamp fixture with a 150 watt flood lamp positioned above the coated screen and positive.

Since the emulsion is sensitive to heat (and these flood lamps generate heat), we suggest you keep the face of the bulb at least 12 inches from the surface of the emulsion. It is important that the image to be photographically transferred to the emulsion receive adequate light, *from edge to edge* of the image. When the bulb or light source is placed very close to the center of a large image, the center, with the correct time, may receive adequate exposure, but the outer areas of the image, further from the light source, might not receive adequate exposure. A general rule for determining light placement to insure adequate edge to edge coverage is to measure the diagonal of the image and place the light at this distance. Since we were working with a small image 10″ x 14″, we set the light 17 inches from the emulsion surface to make our exposure tests. To determine correct exposure, you should do a step-wedge test as described in Chapter III. The exposures made will have areas with two, four, six, eight, ten and twelve minutes of light. After exposure, the positive is peeled away and the screen washed in a warm water spray. Both sides are wet down with the warm water and washed thoroughly. The image will open in the areas masked with the positive that did not receive light.

When the image is thoroughly open, the screen is sprayed on both sides with cold water which will remove any residue and will also harden the photographic emulsion which remains. After a thorough cold water rinse, the screen is placed in front of a fan to dry. When it is thoroughly dry, any open areas (pinholes, etc.) that are not to be printed are blocked in with a water soluble block-out material.

You can now print the test screen following the standard printing procedure. The screen is mounted with the hinges to the printing base. The kick-leg is attached. An ink is selected and printed. By referring to the resulting image, a correct exposure time can be determined.

The test will show that the shorter time exposures are inadequate and fail to thoroughly harden the emulsion. Too much exposure, on the other hand, tends to close up or fill in fine detail. After an exposure time is selected, remove all the ink from the test screen and return the ink to its container. Place several layers of newspaper under the screen and use the proper solvent to remove all traces of the printing ink. Remove the screen from the printing base and wash it with a hot water spray. This spray serves to remove the water soluble block-out and will also soften the photographic emulsion to prepare it for the next operation. Fresh, *full strength* Chlorine bleach, the standard liquid laundry type, is brushed liberally on each surface of the photographic emulsion (both sides alternating). Scrub vigorously with a stiff nylon bristle brush. The screen is allowed to stand for 2–3 minutes (with wet bleach do not allow to dry) and then washed out with hot water, which should remove all traces of the photographic stencil. (It is important that rubber gloves always be worn when using liquid bleach and all containers and brushes should be immediately rinsed with cold water after use.) Since you have determined the correct length of exposure for the light source at the distance selected, you are now ready to prepare a stencil using the previously described coating methods, mounting methods and correct distance and timing. When the screen is thoroughly dry, a water soluble screen filler is used to block out the areas you do not wish to print. When the filler has been thoroughly dried in front of a fan, you mount the screen on the printing base.

TEXTILE PRINTING

In our example the positive used to make the photographic stencil was mounted with masking tape on a "T" shirt. This allows the "T" shirt to be moved under the screen until the stencil image in the screen is in alignment with it.

Screen printing on textiles is much the same as printing on paper. You can apply textile inks to any

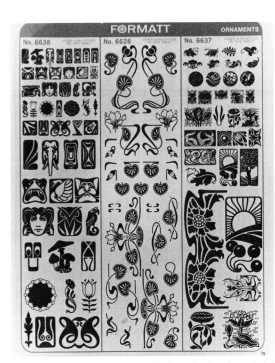

This is a page of ornaments available as dry transfer material manufactured by Formatt. We selected the sunrise symbol for printing on the "T"-shirt.

The letters for RICHARD on the "T"-shirt were chosen from the many rub-down dry transfer type faces available. The letters are Vintage Bold by Prestype.

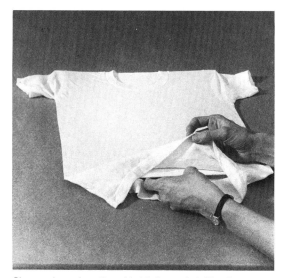

Place a piece of cardboard inside items of clothing that you are printing. This insures that only one thickness will be printed.

Blend. The red ink and the yellow ink were placed into position corresponding to their appearance on the sun.

The two inks (red and yellow) which form the blend are squeegeed exactly as you would a solid color.

natural or synthetic fabrics which can accept 275°–375°F. heat. There are several procedures which must be followed when you screen print on fabric. First, sizing must be removed by washing or it will prevent ink from adhering. When printing items of clothing like a 'T' shirt, place a piece of cardboard inside, as the illustration shows. This insures that only one thickness of the garment will be printed. Because textile inks dry quickly and are permanent, it is absolutley imperative that you clean screens immediately after the printing is completed. Textile inks that are allowed to dry in your screen can be very difficult if not impossible to remove. In order to fix the ink permanently so that it can withstand repeated washing or dry cleaning, it must be heat set. This is accomplished by placing a cloth over the printed area and then ironing each side for 3–5 minutes with a household iron set at medium heat (275°–375°F). Commericaly, these temperatures are achieved through specially designed heat conveyors.

Blends: The sun symbol was printed on the "T"-shirt as a two-color blend. This shading effect can be achieved on paper or most any other flat surface as well as fabric. Remember, that the colors used must be of the same consistency.

The "T"-shirt sun symbol shows a blend which changes from a red orange to a bright yellow. The red ink and the yellow ink were poured into position corresponding to their appearance on the sun. It was squeegeed exactly as if it were a solid color.

To produce a good blending requires printing several proof sheets. When the horizontal demarcation between the colors diminishes to a smooth tonal transition, the blend is ready to be printed. Blends can be made using 3 colors or more following the same procedure.

In our example "T"-shirt we used a sheet of mylar as the flap overlay (pg. 39) to register the second color. We then imprinted RICHARD in blue ink.

The "T"-shirt sun symbol shows a blend which goes from a red-orange to a bright yellow.

PHOTO-POSTERIZATION

Photo-Posterization is basically a rather simple process. The fact that certain high contrast copying films are capable of converting the range of middle tones in a continuous tone image into either black or white makes posterization possible. This film is available under the brand names—Kodak Kodalith; GAF P-407; Agfa Gevalith. It is frequently called Ortho film—referring to the fact that it is orthochromatic, and can be safely processed under a red safelight.

Ortho film either records as full density or fails to record density. This renders intermediate grays invisible. It produces an image with black or white areas. The adjustment of exposure time in the copying process controls the different amounts of black which are produced.

Basically, the system consists of placing a black and white negative in an enlarger or repro-camera. This negative is projection printed several times on several identical size sheets of ortho film, each time using a different length of exposure. All films are developed in the same developer at the same time. As a general rule a minimum of 2½–3 minutes developing time is necessary. Manufacturers' directions regarding length of development and proper developer for the film type should be adhered to strictly. The film with the least exposure will have the largest black area, while increased exposure will develop out with less and less black area. Experiments with exposures and development can be very helpful. The exact exposure times cannot be given, since they will vary with different negatives, light sources, subjects, number of steps, etc. For the screen printer without darkroom equipment or knowledge, posterized positives may be purchased from commercial photographers catering to the printing industry. It is, however, far better for the screen printer to gain experience on his own. This will make it possible to specify requirements clearly, even when purchasing this service.

We have used the negative of a black and white photograph of a Victorian style house. This negative has a density range which extends from the clear film base, which allows approximately 98% of the light falling on it to be transmitted through varying densities that reach a density point which is so opaque that no light can pass. We will separate this image into four values. The negative is placed in an enlarger. It is exposed four times onto four separate sheets of Kodalith film. By using four different lengths of exposure, four different value levels are recorded on the Kodalith film. These four exposures represent four values, seen as different densities in the negative. Each appears as a different percentage of black.

After the posterized positives have been prepared, photographic screens can be made. The enlarger has taken the image apart photographically—we will put that image back together. The four positives and the screens made from those positives represent different percentages of the total area of the image. We will begin this print by printing the screen which represents the largest area. This maximum area screen is actually the lightest value, aside from the paper, that will appear in the final piece. We will print this lightest value in the standard manner.

Before beginning the printing operation, the paper being used is cut to size and a rectangle is drawn on one of these freshly cut sheets. This rectangle, which is the size of the image which will be printed, is centered. This layout sheet allows us to register or "fit" the image being printed to the paper. By placing the layout sheet beneath the screen being used to print, which has already been mounted to the printing base, we can move the paper about until the rectangle lines up with the image in the screen. When registration has been achieved, the layout sheet is taped to the printing base, and the printing guides are attached to the base with masking tape.

We are ready to print; the printing operation is carried out in the usual steps. There are various ways for selecting colors and values of colors used in posterization processes. The simplest choice is a series of gray values. In this system the paper should be considered the lightest value. For our print, we have produced four posterized steps. If we consider

a

b

The original black and white continuous tone photographic negative was used to produce four posterized positives a, b, c, and d. These were made into photographic stencils. If we consider the white of the paper as the lightest value, we see that our image has been created in five steps a, b, c, ending with the darkest gray which approaches a full black d. By selecting three grays a, b, c which approximately divide the white to almost black spectrum into five equal increments, we have created a posterized print. By utilizing this principle of working from light to dark value, this very same image can be printed by substituting a color for gray (p. 36).

the white of the paper as the lightest value, we can say that we are creating an image in five steps ending with the darkest gray which approaches a full black. We have, therefore, selected three other grays which approximately divide the white to almost black spectrum into five equal increments. Our print will consist of four grays plus the white paper.

This image is the result of visual impact based upon the amount of light reflected from a surface.

Another system of colors applied to posterization utilizes this principle of working from light to dark value, with the addition of hue. We have selected a

a + b

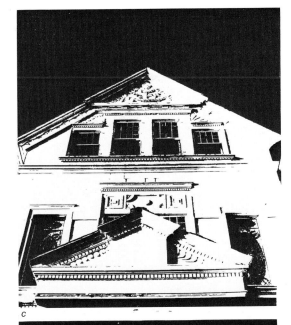

c

a + b + c

d

a + b + c + d

blue with a greenish tint; by adding white to this color, we have produced four values of that blue which range from a very light pastel tint to the original full saturation blue. We are simply working with light to dark value in color.

We have used posterization to depict value changes and value change utilizing one color. A posterized print cannot only display value change and color, but can relate to a segment of the color wheel. The maximum area screen can be used to print a light value yellow green. Through the screen printing the second largest area, we could print a green, slightly darker in value than the first yellow green print. Progressing to the stencil with the next greatest area, we could print a blue green which is slightly darker in value than the second step green. The fourth screen, the smallest printing area, could then be printed using a blue, representing the darkest value. This is called an adjacent color scheme, because the colors fall next to one another in the color wheel and all contain the same primary hue (color). You have probably noticed that all color systems we have described as applicable to posterization, progress through a series of values. The first example moved from the white of the paper through a series of grays to an almost black value gray. The second example was a series of values of one color. The third example employed four different colors whose values formed a progression from light to dark. Knowing that the eye and brain instantly perceive levels of light reflected from objects, we can carefully select a scale of values so that a hue or color can deliver dramatic emphasis to an image. The eye will first record and accept the reality of value levels and then be influenced by the choice of hue or color. There are no rules regarding the use of posterization with hues and values. However, for an understanding of color and value relationships, posterization offers a visual demonstration without parallel.

Unfortunately, it is impossible to reproduce any of the accompanying photographs without the halftone screen dot necesssary for printing this book! This must be considered when they are viewed.

MULTICOLOR PRINT

In general, the procedure for making stencils for multicolor prints is the same as one-color prints. However, registration is essential to the process.

Each color will require an individual stencil except when transparent color is employed to overlap previous color to produce additional colors. It is possible to use one screen for all the colors. However, when a color has been printed, the stencil must be dissolved so that the screen can be used for the next color. If you wish to save the stencils, you will have to use as many screens as colors being printed. Each screen will have to fit the printing base, and all the colors will use the same register guides. Whenever possible, for printing an edition, a separate screen for each stencil should be made. This allows you to proof all the stencils which will reveal the image. You can then manipulate the printing order and make adjustments if you wish. The edition can then be printed with the prepared stencils.

There are no absolute rules by which the order of colors to be printed can be determined. Yet, in multicolor printing it is necessary to decide the sequence of colors before the printing operation can begin. The art work should be carefully analyzed. Bear in mind that the art work can be a drawing, painting, photograph, collage, magazine illustration or comparable visual material. Very often, the sequence would be similar to the way in which you would hand color the image. For this reason we recommend that a layout or maquette of the image be prepared. A full color layout should be scaled to the size of the intended print. Any medium or combination of mediums can be used to work out the number of colors—paint, ink, crayon, colored paper, etc. When this maquette is complete, each color is separated so that it can be made into a stencil. As a guide, the largest and lightest color area may be printed first.

To demonstrate the contemporary possibilities of screen printing, we have produced a collage which will serve as the basis for a multi-color screen print. All the colors will be printed through photographic

Original collage used as the basis for a multi-color screenprint.

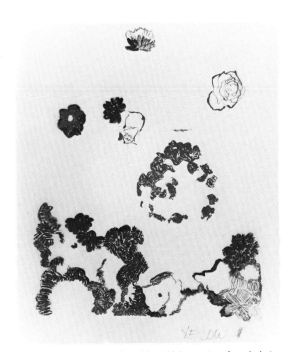

This is the hand-prepared positive which was transferred photographically into a stencil, and then used to print the first color, yellow.

Applying dry transfer border onto prepared acetate as part of second (blue) positive.

Stencil for second color blue was produced from a positive which incorporated a dry transfer material border.

stencils. The methods and materials of the photo-stencil permit the greatest freedom of expression. It is now possible to create a full range of tones, textures and forms with screen printing. The remarkable versatility of screen printing is rapidly being acknowledged. Hard edges and flat opaque colors no longer characterize and limit the screen print.

The artist has first determined the paper size to be used for the print. She has positioned the image to be printed in relation to the four sides of the paper, and marked the intended guide points. This is accomplished by simply placing a sheet of tracing paper of the correct size over the intended image; the outside dimensions of the illustration are then indicated and guide points marked.

The artist has decided to take advantage of the many color possibilities generated by printing trans-parent color over earlier printed color, as well as over areas of the unprinted paper. By using a transparent magic marker to lay in these areas on the layout, the transparent effects can be visualized.

After careful analysis, the artist has determined to print yellow as the first color. The prepared acetate is marked with guide points that are registered with the color layout beneath it. Each color separation must be registered in multicolor work to insure accuracy. The following system is most universally followed:

1) Using pencil or ink, draw a ½ inch crossmark in each of the corners of the original.

2) These crossmarks are duplicated on each pre-pared acetate sheet used to prepare a positive for each color.

3) With each color printed, therefore, the crossmarks will appear as part of the print.

4) A perfectly registered print will show crossmarks coinciding precisely upon previous crossmarks.

The first stencil we will prepare will represent the largest and lightest color we will print. The prepared acetate is placed over the collage and registered to it. Referring to the color layout the artist will work directly on the translucent material. To create textural and tonal variations the artist has used different media. For loose edge qualities an oil crayon was used to translate the quality of embroidery yarn in the collage. Photographer's opaque was painted on with a brush to capture the quality of the candy and candy wrappings. Pen and ink and litho pencil were also used. After the prepared acetate has been imprinted in all areas which will be printed yellow, it is set aside to dry. When dry, it can be transferred into a screen as a stencil. All the steps in direct photo-stencil preparation (pg. 48) must be followed. The first stencil is printed using an opaque yellow ink.

We will print a transparent blue through the second stencil. In addition, this positive incorporates a border. This border was selected from among the numerous commercial dry transfer sheets available. We follow the same procedure for preparing this positive as we did for the first. We will refer to our color layout. We know that we will see blue where it falls on the white of the paper, and we will see green where it falls over the yellow printed as the first color. The prepared acetate is imprinted using various materials. Once more, the image is transferred into a screen photographically. When this screen is ready to print it is mounted on the printing base. The hand-drawn positive used to make the second stencil is mounted on one of the previously printed pieces, so it is in register with the yellow areas already printed. Small pieces of masking tape are used for mounting. This is moved under the screen until the stencil image in the screen is in alignment with the image on the hand-drawn positive. When this has been achieved, the hand-drawn positive is removed and the printed piece is taped with masking tape to the printing base. The guides are taped into position, being certain to use the same three guide points used for earlier printing operation. We now have a situation whereby the screen can be lowered to the printing position and ink squeegeed through it, in correct orientation to the previously printed colors. Sometimes, although the image and printed piece has been registered to one another with great care, some adjustment is still necessary to achieve absolute "fit" or registration. This requires that the piece to be printed be moved slightly to one side or another, up or down. This can only be determined by looking at the first one or two pieces printed. If everything fits, the printing operation continues. If not, the guides must be moved slightly to achieve correct registra-

Hand preparation of a positive; working on prepared acetate. A variety of media have been used—pen and ink, litho crayon, photographer's opaque.

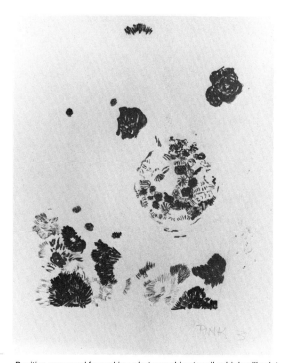

Positive prepared for making photographic stencil, which will print third color, pink.

tion. After visually inspecting the printed piece, the next piece to be printed should be placed on the printing base against the guides, then by referring to the piece just printed, the sheet is shifted accordingly to correct for registration then taped to the printing base. The guides that have to be moved are removed from the printing base and placed against the edge of the next piece to be printed. By some experimentation and manipulation, accurate registration is possible. After we have achieved correct registration we print the second photographic stencil.

The third color we will print will be a transparent pink. The positive is made in the same way as the first two positives.

Following the steps for registering the blue stencil we register this pink stencil. After printing this stencil

we will see pink where it falls on the white of the paper. We will see orange where it falls on the yellow first color, and violet where it falls on the the blue second color. Thus, by printing only three colors we have been able to create six colors.

The first three colors were printed through hand prepared photo-stencils. The next four colors will be printed through stencils which are the result of taking the black and white negative of the original collage and exposing it to produce four posterized positives. These posterized positives are, of course, the same size as the collage. By experimenting with different exposure times (pg. 55) we have finally selected four steps which will add form and contrast to the image. As you will see, posterization need not be an isolated process—it can be used effectively in combination

Original collage and four posterized positives which were produced using the black and white continuous tone negative of the collage.

Halftone positive made from original collage.

with other stencils. We know that a collage image will require textural emphasis of value and tone—the most obvious means for capturing this was to posterize the collage. If we place each of the posterized positives directly on the three-color print we instantly see which areas each will accent. In addition we have carefully selected colors which when printed can further enhance the effect of the posterization. The first and largest posterized step has been printed in transparent Prussian blue. With this step, definition along with texture and color has been brought to the glass jar. In addition it has selectively darkened parts of the image previously printed. The second posterized step has been printed in transparent orange. This warmly intensifies and expands the areas upon which it falls, while balancing the effect of the first cool value step. Thus, the print begins to lose its flat, rather amorphous appearance. The third posterized step is printed in transparent red. While developing the flower forms, it also augments the two larger posterized areas. With these three posterizations we have been able to clarify and bring the image into focus. We know that the last step represents the smallest area and the darkest value. This stencil has been printed in transparent maroon. With this step, the lower picture plane is intensely articulated as an embroidered floral motiff.

HALFTONE PRINTING

To illustrate the methods of making and printing a halftone screen, we have prepared and will print a halftone on our print. For most purposes a halftone positive can be made for you at a repro-photo house.

The halftone positive was produced from the collage that we initially used as our original art. The halftone positive was made the same size as the collage. This halftone positive can be placed on the already printed image for examination, making certain that it fits or "registers."

After checking the halftone positive with the previously printed image, we are ready to make a halftone stencil. The halftone positive being used has a line count of 65 lines per inch. As a "rule of thumb"—the

The artist hand drawing the final positive. This positive is produced by placing the prepared acetate directly over the printed image and creating a line drawing with pen and ink that fits the image printed thus far.

Final hand-drawn positive prepared with pen and ink.

screen fabric used for halftone printing should have three times more the number of threads per linear inch than the line count of the halftone. Because the halftone has 65 lines per inch, we will use a screen fabric with 200 threads per linear inch. Making a halftone stencil is identical to making any other photographic stencil, with one exception. The lines of dots of the halftone must be carefully oriented to the thread direction of the screen fabric to avoid creating unwanted moire patterns (pg. 37).

The easiest way to determine the proper alignment of halftone pattern and screen fabric thread structure is to place the halftone positive in its correct reading position on a lighted surface. The screen can then be placed directly on top of the halftone positive with the screen fabric in contact with the halftone positive. By rotating the screen the moire pattern should be quite apparent.

The object is to rotate the screen in relation to the halftone positive until a position is found where the moire pattern disappears completely or is at a minimum.

When the moire pattern has been minimized, the position of the halftone in relation to the screen should be carefully marked, using a fine tipped Magic Marker directly on the screen fabric. This is done by marking the corners of the positive, or by lightly outlining certain prominent features.

Once more we will note that the screen being used over the halftone positive was thoroughly clean. The screen was washed and then dried prior to alignment with the halftone positive. *Note:* If a backlighted unit is unavailable, the moire pattern can be detected by placing the halftone positive, in the correct reading position, on a piece of clean white cardboard, the screen is placed on the positive and inspected carefully for moire correction.

When the clean screen has been marked for halftone position, the screen is coated with a direct photographic emulsion (as previously described) and left to dry. When dry, the positive is carefully positioned so that it lines up with the marks previously made. Either of the methods described to achieve good contact between the photo-emulsion and the positive can be used. We have used the spray-adhesive method.

For absolute accuracy, a step wedge exposure (pg. 27) could be made. However, for a 65 line halftone, which is a relatively coarse line count, we will give the positive emulsion combination an exposure of 3 minutes from a distance of 17", which we have determined to be the average exposure time according to the step wedge test. The stencil is exposed to light, the positive removed, and the image thoroughly washed with warm water until the halftone image is completely open. The openness of the image can be checked by holding the wet screen up to a strong light source and looking through the screen at the light.

If the image is clean, the screen is sprayed with cold water thoroughly on both sides to slightly harden the emulsion. The screen is dried in front of a fan. When dry, the areas between the image and the screen frame and any other spots or pinholes not intended for printing are filled in using a water soluble screen filler if oil based inks are to be used. The screen filler is dried in front of a fan. Before mounting the screen on the printing base, the underside of the screen fabric is wiped down with paper towels and mineral spirits. This will remove any residue left by the spray adhesive used to mount the positive. The screen is wiped dry and mounted on the printing base. The halftone positive is taped directly to one of the printed pieces. The piece with the halftone positive mounted is placed under the halftone stencil and moved about until the stencil image is in register with the halftone positioned below it.

When alignment is achieved, the printed piece with

the halftone positive is taped lightly to the printing base. The guide points are taped to the printing base making contact with the edge of the sheet to be printed.

It is of utmost importance that the guide points used for the halftone printing be in the same positions used for the previous colors.

Now, a word or two about the ink to be used. While ordinary screen ink can be used, some difficulty may be encountered because of fine dots or details closing up and preventing the ink's passage. Most screen ink manufacturers produce a product known as halftone base. This is a clear or translucent substance with a buttery consistency. Halftone base is used in combination with the screening color. The color and base are thoroughly mixed. The halftone base will help keep the halftone stencil image open thereby allowing it to be printed. The best method we have found for mixing the base and ink is to start with the base and add approximately 25% or ¼ by volume of the color. Mix these two thoroughly. When thoroughly mixed, print a trial proof by printing the image on 3-4 sheets of newsprint. This gets the ink moving through the screen. Then place one of the previously printed pieces on the printing base against the guides and print a proof. Inspect this proof for color quality. If the color is too weak, more color can be added to the mixture already made, thereby increasing its color saturation. On the other hand, if the color is too strong, more halftone base can be added. By manipulating halftone base and color proportions, a very delicate color control is exercised. When the color is correct, the image can be printed. It is important to look carefully at every fourth or fifth impression printed to be certain that the fine halftone dots are not clogging up or "drying-in." If you observe that the fine dots are not printing, the stencil should be given a thorough wash with the proper solvent for the ink being used. With all things in order, we proceed in printing the halftone in the blue gray.

All that remains to complete this print is to print the final hand drawn positive. The artist has created a line drawing in pen and ink. This hand prepared positive is produced by placing a piece of prepared acetate directly over the printed image and drawing with pen and ink. This positive is made into a photographic stencil, and is registered and printed in the exact same way as all the other stencils. The only difference is that this last color, green, has been printed with enamel ink. This ink's gloss and density lends dramatic highlight and surface contrast to the finished print.

THE EDITION

After the printing is complete, the prints to be included in the edition are selected. The number of prints in an edition is an individual decision. In the past, edition size was kept small in order to insure the value of each print and to raise its price as an edition sold out or an artist's fame increased. We must understand that while rarity may make something cost more, it does not necessarily make it superior. This does not alter the fact that for some people there is undeniable pleasure in simply owning something rare. To be realistic, the notion of "limited" must be viewed in its contemporary context. Editions of 200–300 prints are not unusual. In fact, editions of 1,000 and more have been produced. This certainly can qualify as "rare" in relation to a world population of three billion. Consider that it has been estimated that $\frac{1}{6}$ of all people ever born are alive today and you will understand how difficult it is to prognosticate on supply and demand regarding the size of an edition of prints.

After the prints are completely dry, the artist inspects each in order to eliminate those that should not be included in the edition. Usually 10% of those printed are rejected. But this number can be higher, particularly for the beginning printer. The prints in an edition should be identical duplicates. Bear in mind, that even with the most stringent printing controls, minute variations occur from print to print, but these are inconsequential. Damaged, torn, creased and dirt-marked prints are automatically eliminated. In addition, prints with noticeable faults should be re-

Completed print. Each print in the edition is signed and numbered in pencil. The title is written on the left, the artist's signature is on the right. In an edition of fifteen prints, $\frac{1}{15}$ is written on the first print, $\frac{2}{15}$ on the second, this is continued until the last print is numbered, $\frac{15}{15}$.

jected, as well as any that visually deviate from the others. Those prints which remain comprise the edition. Each print in the edition should be numbered and signed in pencil on the bottom margin. The tile of the print usually appears in the left hand corner, the artist's signature in the right and the number in the center. The individual number assigned to a print is useful for record keeping. Since the order in which screen prints have been printed does not have the importance it does for the intaglio or lithograph, the

Artist's Proofs should amount to no more than 10% of the edition. They are signed and numbered, using Roman numerals as above.

assigning of numbers is really arbitrary. As an example, in an edition of 15, each print is assigned a number consecutively, starting from 1 through 15. Each number is followed by a slash and then the total number is the edition—for example 1/15 would be written on the first print in an edition of 15; 2/15 on the second in an edition of 15; this process would continue on each print until all prints through 15/15 had been numbered. Traditionally, a small number of prints of the same quality as those in the numbered edition have been retained by the artist. These are designated as Artist's Proofs and should amount to

no more than 10% of the edition. Artist's Proofs are signed and numbered, however, Roman numerals are used—I/V to V/V.

Signing and numbering prints are today a part of printmaking documentation. Its function has evolved over several centuries. Signatures on prints began to appear in the middle of the 15th Century, where we find them as monogrammed initials used to mark woodcuts and engravings. The famous Durer monogram is a typical example. Engravings made by printers from paintings or drawings of others usually showed two names. At the bottom left hand side is the painter's name followed by a Latin abbreviation certifying that the work is his—for example—pinxit or delineavit are shortened to pinx., delin., or del. The engraver's name appears as sculps., or sc., i nc., abbreviations of sculpsit, incisit which means "has engraved" or fecit—"has made." All these signature forms were engraved in reverse on the plate in order to read correctly when printed. With the advent of lithography, the artist began to use his own handwriting to sign the plate directly so that after it had been printed it was reversed. The reason for this is the virtual impossibility of writing a personal signature in reverse. A signature on a plate became an indication of certainty that it had been made by the artist. On the other hand, it gave the unscrupulous printer carte blanche to print as many impressions as he wished. To guard against indiscriminate reproduction, numbering was adopted. A lithograph printed with a correct reading signature or date indicated a reproduction. For instance, it is easy to distinguish transfer reproductions from original Picasso lithographs by their dating. When Picasso worked on the stone he wrote the date in it, so these prints show the date in reverse on the print; whereas transfer reproductions show the date reading correctly.

With increased interest in prints, it became necessary to find a more reliable means of documenting the originality of a work. Numbering tells the collector the total number of copies of a particular print. It also hinders forgeries which must in addition to a signature have a number within a series. By handsigning a

print, an artist is guaranteeing that it qualifies as an original work of art. He is also authenticating the total number to which the edition has been limited and affirming his approval of the specific print. As a guide, the Print Council of America in their booklet "What is an Original Print" has set forth the following criteria for original graphics:

1) The artist alone has created the master image in or upon the plate, stone, wood block or other material, for the purpose of creating a work of graphic art.

2) The print is made directly from the said material by the artist or pursuant to his directions.

3) The finished print is approved by the artist.

After the edition and the Artist's Proofs have been signed and numbered, all other prints should be destroyed. When progressive proofs of the individual stencils or stencil stages have been retained, they should be so labelled.

While keeping track of one or two prints is quite simple, the best way to maintain a history and status record is to comprehensively inventory prints from the very first edition. Using a ruled notebook for this purpose, enter all the details of an edition—date(s) of printing, title, number of colors, materials used, along with other pertinent technical information. Following this biographical history, list the number of each print in the edition allowing two or three lines for each one. Here, enter information and dates regarding prices, sales, names and addresses of buyers, loans, exhibitions, data related to mounting, matting and framing.

Prints should be stored flat. If stacked vertically the paper tends to slacken and ripple. Rolling for storage can loosen ink and cause flaking. Keeping a print rolled can also make presenting it flat very difficult. If it is necessary to ship a print in a mailing tube, roll it to no less than a 4″ diameter, and cover the printed surface with tissue.

Works of art on paper are subject to deterioration and damage from a number of causes, including excessive heat and light, air pollutants and extreme humidity. Art on paper can be affected by such environmental conditions, as well as prolonged contact with chemically unstable materials such as those found in most cardboards.

Although matting and framing are assumed to be ways of protecting as well as displaying prints, the fact is that if improper materials are used this does more harm than good.

1) **Mounting & Matting**—The only safe board for these procedures is 100% rag stock, which is pH neutral. Any other stock is likely to be nothing more than cardboard with a core of groundwood which will eventually deteriorate and consequently stain the paper it touches. Therefore, mount and mat with 100% ragboard pH neutral—not board with only a rag paper layer on its surface. We suggest 4-ply ragboard.

2) **Matting & Hinging**—A print should *never* be glued directly to a backboard (mount). Nor should *it* be directly attached to the window, or mat. The generally accepted method of matting involves a mount and a mat. The work of art is hinged to the mount, in upper corners only, with rectangular pieces of Japanese mulberry paper which are folded so that half the rectangle is on the mount and half on the object, thus creating a hinge. In addition, a method which precludes any glue from contacting the paper is to make a mulberry or rag paper envelope corner in which each corner of the print can be set. In either case the adhesive should be a vegetable based paste. Never use synthetic adhesives like rubber cement, since most will stain paper. Self-adhering tapes, whether masking or "scotch" will stain almost immediately. Gummed linen tape which is employed by many framers will cause yellowing in time. Although it is generally the rear surface which shows such effect, in the case of thin papers, the stain will bleed through to the front. The one notable commercial hinging material which does not seem to stain is a gummed glassine paper supplied in sheets by the Dennison Manufacturing Company. Mounts should be somewhat larger than the art work itself, so that the art object's edges cannot touch a frame. Remember, mounts and mats covered with natural silk or linen are harmless only if the board underneath is of 100% rag content, with neutral pH.

3) **Glazing & Sealing**—For protection from dirt and other pollutants while on display, a print should *always* be framed under glass or rigid plastic, such as Plexiglas. The print, however, should *never* touch the glass. The inside of the glass is subject to moisture and condensation which is transferred to the paper when there is no space between the glass and the print. A sufficiently thick mat is a common solution to the problem of separation.

Whether or not the closed frame should be sealed against air leaks or be allowed to breathe is a debatable question. Conservators disagree on any general rule. However, in areas of high pollution, sealing is probably desirable. This is done by running a continuous strip of transparent self-adhering tape along the edges of the glass after the back is covered with aluminum foil or a polyethylene sheet.

HANGING

Light: Sunlight, direct and indirect, as well as fluorescent lighting are rich in ultra-violet rays and are, therefore, harmful to paper. Rooms where prints are hung should be weak in sunlight and illuminated by relatively harmless incandescent lighting. While use of ultraviolet filter Plexiglas can reduce light damage, it is nevertheless advisable, wherever possible, to avoid direct sunlight and fluorescent light.

Heat: Never hang works of art near radiators or other sources of heat nor on flue-containing walls.

Humidity: 70% is the maximum safe relative humidity for paper. Above this level, one risks mildewing the paper. Avoid hanging works of art in such areas unless dehumidified or air conditioned. Nor should they be hung on damp walls. Dry conditions, below 30% relative humidity, can cause brittleness and should likewise be avoided wherever possible.

In creating a screen print the artist must make many crucial decisions. Inevitably, the intensely satisfying process of producing a print is completed. The decision to stop is made when an artist realizes that to continue will spoil rather than enhance a project. We believe this is true of a book, as well. An author, too, must exercise judgmental discrimination by recognizing that the time to close has come.

INDEX